Verse by Verse Commentary on

ECCLESIASTES

AND

SONG OF SOLOMON

Enduring Word Commentary Series

By David Guzik

The grass withers, the flower fades,
but the word of our God stands forever.
Isaiah 40:8

Commentary on Ecclesiastes and Song of Solomon

Copyright ©2019 by David Guzik

Printed in the United States of America
or in the United Kingdom

Print Edition ISBN: 978-1-939466-23-5

Enduring Word

5662 Calle Real #184

Goleta, CA 93117

Electronic Mail: ewm@enduringword.com

Internet Home Page: www.enduringword.com

Scripture references, unless noted, are from the New King James Version of the Bible, copyright ©1979, 1980, 1982, Thomas Nelson, Inc., Publisher.

Contents

Ecclesiastes 1 - The Vanity of Life

A. Introduction: The Preacher, the author of Ecclesiastes.

1. (1a) The Preacher.

The words of the Preacher,

a. **The words of the Preacher**: The Book of Ecclesiastes is one of the most unusual and perhaps most difficult to understand books of the Bible. It has a spirit of hopeless despair; it has no praise or peace; it seems to promote questionable conduct. Yet these **words of the Preacher** show us the futility and foolishness of a life lived without an eternal perspective.

i. The question in Ecclesiastes isn't about the existence of God; the author is no atheist, and God is always there. The question is whether or not God *matters*. The answer to that question is vitally connected to a responsibility to God that goes beyond this earthly life.

ii. "He does believe in 'God,' but, very significantly, he never uses the sacred name 'Lord.' He has shaken himself free, or wishes to represent a character who has shaken himself free from Revelation, and is fighting the problem of life, its meaning and worth, without any help from Law, or Prophet, or Psalm." (Maclaren)

iii. In the search for this answer, **the Preacher** searched the depths of human experience, including despair. He thoroughly examined the emptiness and futility of life lived *without* eternity before coming to the conclusion of the necessity of eternity.

iv. "We face the appalling inference that nothing has meaning, nothing matters under the sun. It is then that we can hear, as the good news which it is, that *everything* matters – 'for God will bring every deed into judgment, with every secret thing, whether good or evil.'" (Kidner)

v. "What, then, is the purpose of Ecclesiastes? It is an essay in apologetics. It defends the life of faith in a generous God by pointing to the grimness of the alternative." (Eaton)

vi. "He does not come as a formal philosopher; it is a word from God he has to share, despite his reflective low-key approach. He does not present half-a-dozen arguments for the existence of God. Instead he picks up our own questions. Can you cope with life without having any idea where you are going? You don't have all the answers to life's enigmas, do you? Your neo-pagan view of life doesn't give you any hope of achieving very much, does it? Nature will not answer your questions, and you are bored by it anyway. History baffles your attempts to understand it. You don't like to think about your own death; yet it is the most certain fact about your existence." (Eaton)

vii. "Ecclesiastes does not pretend to preach the Gospel. Rather, it encourages the reader to a God-centered worldview rather than falling victim to frustrations and unanswered questions. None of its contents has to be rejected in the light of the New Testament." (Wright)

b. **The Preacher**: In Hebrew, this translates the word *Koheleth* (or, *Kobellet*). The idea is of someone who might gather, lead, or speak to a group of people – a congregation.

i. "The word is connected with the Hebrew for assembling, and its form suggests some kind of office-bearer.... The many attempts at translating this title include: 'Ecclesiastes', 'The Preacher', 'The Speaker', 'The President', 'The Spokesman', 'The Philosopher'. We might almost add, 'The Professor'!" (Kidner)

ii. These are definitely the **words of the Preacher**, but in this apologetically oriented sermon his focus on God is indirect. "It makes no mention of Yahweh, the LORD, the name of the God of Israel's covenant faith. It scarcely refers to the law of God, the only possible reference being in 12:13. It scarcely refers to the nation of Israel (only in 1:12). Why these omissions? The answer seems to be that the Preacher's argument stands on its own feet and does not depend on Israel's covenant faith to be valid. He is appealing to universally observable facts." (Eaton)

2. (1b) The identity of the Preacher.

The son of David, king in Jerusalem.

a. **The son of David**: This identifies the Preacher as David's son, Solomon. Some believe that another wrote it in Solomon's name, but there is no compelling reason to say that anyone other than Solomon wrote it.

i. "In view of the traditions concerning Solomon (1 Kings 2-12; 2 Chronicles 1-9), without any further definition the title would certainly lead any reader to suppose that the allusion is to him. Also the account in 2:1-11 is strongly reminiscent of Solomon; almost every phrase has its parallel in the narratives concerning Solomon." (Eaton)

ii. "There will come another enigmatic note in verse 16, with its claim to a wisdom 'surpassing all who were over Jerusalem before me'. This rules out any successor to the matchless Solomon." (Kidner)

b. **King in Jerusalem**: From his royal standing, Solomon had the wisdom, freedom, resources, and standing to write this work.

i. In a sense, *only* Solomon could write this book. He had both the wisdom and the resources to work through these problems. "With Qoheleth we put on the mantle of a Solomon, that most brilliant and least limited of men, to set out on the search. With every gift and power at our command, it would be strange if we should come back empty-handed." (Kidner)

ii. When Solomon wrote this, he did so in a style understood and appreciated in his day. "The particular brand of wisdom that characterizes Ecclesiastes is well attested in the ancient world. We may call it 'pessimism literature'. Ecclesiastes is the only biblical example of this old literary tradition." (Eaton)

iii. "In an Egyptian work, *The Man Who Was Tired of Life*, written between 2300 and 2100 BC, a man disputed with his soul whether life was worth living or whether suicide was the only logical act. 'Life is a transitory state,' he complained to himself; 'you are alive but what profit do you get? Yet you yearn for life like a man of wealth.' Death is 'a bringer of weeping'; never again afterwards will a man 'see the sun'. Little can be done. 'Follow the happy day and forget care.'" (Eaton)

iv. The Puritan commentator John Trapp wrote what some other also believe, that Ecclesiastes was Solomon's statement of error and penance, and evidence that he turned back to God at the end of his life – despite the absence of such assurance in 1 Kings 11. "He penned this penitential sermon, grown an old man, he had experimented all this that he here affirmeth, so that he might better begin his speech to his scholars." (Trapp)

B. The problem presented: the meaninglessness of life.

1. (2) The Preacher's summary: Life is vanity, without meaning.

"Vanity of vanities," says the Preacher;
"Vanity of vanities, all *is* vanity."

a. **Vanity of vanities**: The Preacher begins his sermon with his first conclusion (though not his ultimate conclusion). Looking at life all around, he judges it to be **vanity** – nothing, useless, meaningless.

i. "A wisp of vapour, a puff of wind, a mere breath – nothing you could get your hands on; the nearest thing to zero. That is the 'vanity' this book is about." (Kidner)

ii. "*Vanity (hebel)* includes (i) brevity and unsubstantiality, *emptiness...* (ii) unreliability, frailty...(iii) futility, as in Job 9:29 (Hebrew), where 'in vanity' means 'to no effect'; (iv) deceit (*cf.* Jeremiah 16:19; Zechariah 10:2)." (Eaton)

b. **Vanity of vanities**: To strengthen his point, the Preacher judged life to be *the ultimate* vanity, the **vanity of vanities**. This Hebrew phrasing is used to express intensity or the ultimate of something, as in the phrase *holy of holies*.

i. This phrase (or something quite like it) will be used about 30 times in this short book. It is one of the major themes of Ecclesiastes.

c. **All is vanity**: To further strengthen the point, Solomon noted not only that life is **vanity**, but that **all is vanity**. It seemed that every part of life suffered from this emptiness.

i. We see from the first two verses that Solomon wrote this from a certain perspective, a perspective that through the book he will expose as inadequate and wrong. Most all of Ecclesiastes is written from this perspective, through the eyes of a man who thinks and lives as if God doesn't matter.

ii. "It is an absolutely accurate statement of life when it is lived under certain conditions; but it is not true as a statement of what life must necessarily be." (Morgan) If you say, "My life isn't vanity; it isn't meaningless. My life is filled with meaning and purpose." That's wonderful; but you can't ignore the premise of the Preacher – the premise of life *under the sun*.

iii. Therefore Ecclesiastes is filled with what we might call true lies. Given the perspective "God does not matter," it is true that **all is vanity**. Since that perspective is wrong, it *is not true* that **all is vanity**. Yet Solomon makes us think through this wrong perspective thoroughly through Ecclesiastes.

iv. Solomon thinks through this perspective, but he wasn't the first nor the last to see life this way. Many moderns judge life to be equally futile.

- "We all live in a house on fire, no fire department to call; no way out, just the upstairs window to look out of while the fire burns the house down with us trapped, locked in it." (Playwright Tennessee Williams)
- "Most people get a fair amount of fun out of their lives, but on balance life is suffering and only the very young or the very foolish imagine otherwise." (Author George Orwell)
- "Life is rather like a can of sardines, we're all of us looking for the key." (Playwright Alan Bennett)

2. (3) Life and work **under the sun**.

What profit has a man from all his labor
In which he toils under the sun?

a. **What profit has a man from all his labor**: Using the language from the world of business, the Preacher asked a worthy question. He knew that life was filled with **labor** – but what is it worth? What does it **profit**?

i. **Profit**: "A commercial term; life 'pays no dividends'." (Eaton)

ii. Jesus expressed a similar thought in Mark 8:36: *For what will it profit a man if he gains the whole world, and loses his own soul?*

iii. "All things are sweeter in the ambition than in the fruition. There is a singular vanity in this splendid misery." (Trapp)

b. **In which he toils under the sun**: This is the first stating of an essential theme through Ecclesiastes. This phrase will be repeated more than 25 times through the book. The idea isn't "on a sunny day" or something having to do with the weather. The idea is "in this world that we can see; the material world." It is life considered *without* an eternal perspective.

i. "If our view of life goes no further than 'under the sun', all our endeavours will have an undertone of misery." (Eaton)

ii. The use of the phrase **under the sun** "shows that the writer's interest was universal and not limited to only his own people and land." (Wright)

3. (4-7) The unending cycle of creation.

One generation passes away, and *another* generation comes;
But the earth abides forever.
The sun also rises, and the sun goes down,
And hastens to the place where it arose.
The wind goes toward the south,
And turns around to the north;

The wind whirls about continually,
And comes again on its circuit.
All the rivers run into the sea,
Yet the sea *is* not full;
To the place from which the rivers come,
There they return again.

a. **One generation passes away, and another generation comes; but the earth abides forever**: Using several examples, the Preacher observes that nothing seems to change very much in the seemingly unending cycle of nature.

i. "He looks out upon humanity, and sees that in one aspect the world is full of births, and in another full of deaths. Coffins and cradles seem the main furniture, and he hears the tramp, tramp, tramp of the generations passing over a soil honeycombed with tombs." (Maclaren)

b. **The sun also rises.... The wind goes toward the south...the rivers run into the sea**: From what Solomon could observe *under the sun*, these unchanging cycles expressed the unchanging monotony of life, leading to its vanity and meaninglessness.

i. "For Old Testament orthodoxy, creation rings with the praises of the LORD. Creation is his.... But, says the Preacher, take away its God, and creation no longer reflects his glory; it illustrates the weariness of mankind." (Eaton)

ii. "All the rivers of earthly joy may be flowing into your heart, but they will never fill it. They may recede, or dry up, or ebb; but if not, still they will never satisfy.... But in Christ there is perennial interest.... We need not go outside of Him for new delights; and to know Him is to possess a secret which makes all things new." (Meyer)

4. (8-11) The unending cycle of man's labor.

All things *are* full of labor;
Man cannot express *it*.
The eye is not satisfied with seeing,
Nor the ear filled with hearing.
That which has been *is* what will be,
That which *is* done is what will be done,
And *there is* nothing new under the sun.
Is there anything of which it may be said,
"See, this *is* new"?
It has already been in ancient times before us.
There is no remembrance of former *things*,

**Nor will there be any remembrance of *things* that are to come
By *those* who will come after.**

a. **All things are full of labor; man cannot express it**: Solomon then observed that the meaninglessness of life wasn't only reflected in nature. This frustration is also evident in human effort and endeavor. Despite all man's working (**labor**), **seeing**, and **hearing**, he is still **not satisfied**.

i. "It is impossible to calculate how much anxiety, pain, labour, and fatigue are necessary in order to carry on the *common operations of life*. But an *endless desire of gain*, and an *endless curiosity* to *witness* a variety of results, cause men to, labour on." (Clarke)

ii. "What is the difference between a squirrel in a cage who only makes his prison go round the faster by his swift race, and the man who lives toilsome days for transitory objects which he may never attain?" (Maclaren)

b. **That which has been is what will be, that which is done is what will be done, and there is nothing new under the sun**: Despite all man's work and progress, life seems monotonously the same. Things that seem new get old very quickly, so it could be said "**there is nothing new under the sun.**"

i. The more things change, the more they stay the same. Meet the new boss, same as the old boss. "In their new guise the old ways go on. As a race, we never learn." (Kidner)

ii. There may be **nothing new under the sun**; but thankfully the followers of Jesus – those born again by God's Spirit – don't live **under the sun** in that sense. Their life is filled with new things.

- A new name (Isaiah 62:2, Revelation 2:17).
- A new community (Ephesians 2:14).
- A new help from angels (Psalm 91:11).
- A new commandment (John 13:34).
- A new covenant (Jeremiah 31:33, Matthew 26:28).
- A new and living way to heaven (Hebrews 10:20).
- A new purity (1 Corinthians 5:7).
- A new nature (Ephesians 4:24).
- A new creation in Jesus Christ (2 Corinthians 5:17).
- All things become new! (2 Corinthians 5:17, Revelation 21:5).

c. **There is no remembrance of former things, nor will there be any remembrance of things that are come**: The futility of life seems to extend in both directions, both into the past and into the future. Man works hard, yet it never seems to make a lasting difference and all is simply forgotten.

> i. "How many memorable matters were never recorded! How many ancient records long since perished!" (Trapp)

C. The failure of wisdom to satisfy.

1. (12-15) Searching by wisdom.

I, the Preacher, was king over Israel in Jerusalem. And I set my heart to seek and search out by wisdom concerning all that is done under heaven; this burdensome task God has given to the sons of man, by which they may be exercised. I have seen all the works that are done under the sun; and indeed, all *is* vanity and grasping for the wind.

What is crooked cannot be made straight,
And what is lacking cannot be numbered.

> a. **I, the Preacher, was king over Israel in Jerusalem**: Solomon was internationally famous for his great wisdom. If the answers to the seeming emptiness of life could be found by wisdom, Solomon was the one to find them.

>> i. Solomon's great wisdom was a gift of God. When God offered him whatever he pleased, he asked for wisdom, especially the wisdom to lead the people of God (1 Kings 3:5-28). Therefore, God made Solomon so wise that he wrote thousands of proverbs, and he was considered to be wiser than all the men of his day (1 Kings 4:29-34).

> b. **I set my heart to seek and search out by wisdom concerning all that is done under heaven**: With the unique ability to make such a search, Solomon looked for the answers in **wisdom** – by which he meant human wisdom that *excluded* answers in the light of eternity.

>> i. **I set my heart to seek and search out**: "The two words are not synonymous. The former verb implies penetrating into the depth of an object before one; the other word taking a comprehensive survey of matters further away; so that two methods and scopes of investigation are signified." (Deane)

>> ii. This is the wisdom of those who guide us to a better life in the here-and-now; how to live a healthier, happier, more prosperous life. This wisdom certainly has value, and many lives would be better for following it. Yet if it excludes a true appreciation of eternity and our responsibilities in the world to come, this wisdom has no true answer to the meaninglessness of life. It only shows us how to live our meaningless lives *better*.

iii. In other places in Ecclesiastes, **wisdom** is thought of as a blessing – as it is; even wisdom that excludes eternity (Ecclesiastes 7:11-12, 7:19). Yet this kind of **under the sun** wisdom cannot shed light upon the problem of the vanity and meaninglessness of life.

c. **All that is done under heaven**: *God's* heaven and eternity are not in view here, only the day and night skies. This is another way of saying, "**under the sun**." All man's work, accomplishment, and searching for wisdom seems to amount to nothing.

i. "*All that is done under heaven* shows that the total resources of a limited world-view are the object of study; the vertical aspect is not yet in view." (Eaton)

d. **This burdensome task God has given to the sons of man, by which they may be exercised**: The seeming futility of life *comes from God*; He **has given** it to man. God has deliberately built a system where life seems meaningless and empty without the understanding of a living, active God to whom we must give account.

i. It may seem cruel of God to devise such a system, but it is actually evidence of His great love and mercy. He built within us the desire and need for that which brings meaning and fulfillment to life. As Augustine wrote, the Creator made a God-shaped space in each of us, which can only be filled with Him.

ii. This desire is found not only in us as people, but also in creation itself. God also subjected creation to this futility until He one day brings the promised fulfillment. *For the creation was subjected to futility, not willingly, but because of Him who subjected it in hope* (Romans 8:20).

iii. At the same time, this is a **burdensome task**. It isn't always easy to find these answers because our pride, self-reliance, and self-love work against finding them.

e. **What is crooked cannot be made straight, and what is lacking cannot be numbered**: The Preacher's initial search for the answers in wisdom (under the sun) brought him only despair.

i. "With his usual devastating candour Qoheleth is quick to tell us the worst. The search has come to nothing." (Kidner)

ii. "The third conclusion explains why the 'under the sun' thinker is so frustrated. It is because there are twists (*what is crooked*) and gaps (*what is lacking*) in all thinking. No matter how the thinker ponders, he cannot straighten out life's anomalies, nor reduce all he sees to a neat system." (Eaton)

2. (16-18) The failure of wisdom confirmed.

I communed with my heart, saying, "Look, I have attained greatness, and have gained more wisdom than all who were before me in Jerusalem. My heart has understood great wisdom and knowledge." And I set my heart to know wisdom and to know madness and folly. I perceived that this also is grasping for the wind.

For in much wisdom *is* much grief,
And he who increases knowledge increases sorrow.

a. **I communed with my heart**: This approach is natural for anyone who looks for the answers *under the sun*, apart from an eternal perspective. They look *inward* for wisdom and answers, instead of to the God who rules eternity.

b. **I set my heart to know wisdom and to know madness and folly. I perceived that this also is grasping for the wind**: The repeated and intensified search for wisdom brought no ultimate meaning. The solution wasn't to think harder and search better; it was all **grasping for the wind**.

c. **For in much wisdom is much grief, and he who increases knowledge increases sorrow**: The more the Preacher understood life *under the sun*, the greater his despair. The more he learned, the more he realized what he *didn't* know. The more he knew, the more he knew life's sorrows.

i. "So long as wisdom is restricted to the realm 'under the sun', it sees the throbbing tumult of creation, life scurrying round its ever-repetitive circuits, and nothing more. 'The more you understand, the more you ache' (Moffatt)." (Eaton)

Ecclesiastes 2 - Life in View of Death

A. The pursuit of pleasure tested – and found lacking.

1. (1) The summary.

I said in my heart, "Come now, I will test you with mirth; therefore enjoy pleasure"; but surely, this also *was* vanity.

a. **I said in my heart, "Come now, I will test you"**: The previous section saw Solomon look for the meaning of life in wisdom – wisdom as it can be understood *apart* from eternity. He found no meaning in skillful, wise living *under the sun*. Now he continued his search for meaning and tested a life of pleasure and amusement.

i. "The Preacher is not testing pleasure so much as himself." (Eaton)

b. **Come now, I will test you with mirth; therefore enjoy pleasure**: Solomon tested life's meaning in **mirth** and **pleasure**. He tested the theory many live under today; that the meaning of life is found in more and varied pleasures, entertainments, and excitements.

c. **But surely, this also was vanity**: The Preacher will shortly explain how he came to this conclusion; but he tells us the result of the testing at the beginning.

2. (2-3) The search for meaning in pleasure.

I said of laughter–"Madness!"; and of mirth, "What does it accomplish?" I searched in my heart *how* to gratify my flesh with wine, while guiding my heart with wisdom, and how to lay hold on folly, till I might see what *was* good for the sons of men to do under heaven all the days of their lives.

a. **I said of laughter – "Madness!"; and of mirth, "What does it accomplish"**: Solomon tested the life lived for laughter, pleasure, and fun. Like a modern celebrity he ran from party to party, entertainment to entertainment. At the end of it all, he judged it to be **"Madness"** and without accomplishment.

> i. **Laughter**: "A superficial gaiety, used of the 'fun' of a game (Proverbs 1:23) or a party (Ecclesiastes 10:19), or the 'derision' which Jeremiah suffered (Jeremiah 20:7)." (Eaton)

> ii. **Mirth**: "Thoughtful pleasure, the joy of religious festivals (Numbers 10:10, Judges 16:23), gratitude in serving the LORD (Deuteronomy 28:47), or the proclamation of a king (1 Kings 1:40)." (Eaton)

> iii. Yet, Eaton is careful to add that "the distinction cannot always be sharply drawn."

> iv. Clarke on **laughter** and **mirth**: "He tells the *former* to her face that *she is mad*; but as to the *latter*, he thinks her so much beneath his notice, that he only points at her, and instantly turns his back."

b. **I searched in my heart how to gratify my flesh with wine…and how to lay hold on folly**: The Preacher lived a life satiated with the pleasures of wine and light, frivolous amusements. He wanted to **see what was good for the sons of men to do** if this life was all there was.

3. (4-8) The search for meaning in work and accomplishments.

I made my works great, I built myself houses, and planted myself vineyards. I made myself gardens and orchards, and I planted all *kinds* of fruit trees in them. I made myself water pools from which to water the growing trees of the grove. I acquired male and female servants, and had servants born in my house. Yes, I had greater possessions of herds and flocks than all who were in Jerusalem before me. I also gathered for myself silver and gold and the special treasures of kings and of the provinces. I acquired male and female singers, the delights of the sons of men, *and* musical instruments of all kinds.

a. **I made my works great**: The Preacher looked not only for meaning in amusements, but also in great and legitimate accomplishments. He tried to give life meaning through the satisfaction that comes through building and organizing and improving one's environment.

> i. "As if he had over-reacted in turning to futile pleasures, he now gives himself to the joys of creativity." (Kidner)

b. **Gardens and orchards…male and female servants…herds and flocks… silver and gold**: If building, improving, and amassing great riches and accomplishments could give true meaning to life, the Preacher would have found it.

i. **Special treasures of kings and of the provinces**: "1. The *taxes* levied off his subjects. 2. The *tribute* given by the neighboring potentates. Both these make the 'peculiar treasure of kings;' *taxes* and *tribute*." (Clarke)

ii. **Musical instruments of all kinds**: "The final item in the list may well refer to Solomon's wives and concubines, but the Hebrew word does not occur elsewhere in the Bible." (Wright) The NIV translates, "Harem" and the RSV "Concubines." The word might be related to the Hebrew word for *breast*. According to Wright, a Canaanite word of similar form is used to translate the Egyptian word for "concubine." However, the traditional Jewish rendering is **musical instruments**.

4. (9-11) The analysis from the search.

So I became great and excelled more than all who were before me in Jerusalem. Also my wisdom remained with me.

Whatever my eyes desired I did not keep from them.
I did not withhold my heart from any pleasure,
For my heart rejoiced in all my labor;
And this was my reward from all my labor.
Then I looked on all the works that my hands had done
And on the labor in which I had toiled;
And indeed all *was* vanity and grasping for the wind.
***There was* no profit under the sun.**

a. **So I became great and excelled more than all who were before me in Jerusalem**: Solomon's accomplishments rightly lifted him to prominence, and he had whatever meaning *fame* could bring to life.

b. **Also my wisdom remained with me**: In all of this Solomon did not lose his wisdom or ability to genuinely assess meaning and fulfillment – at least in an *under the sun* sense.

c. **Whatever my eyes desired I did not keep from them. I did not withhold my heart from any pleasure**: This is even more significant coming from Solomon, who had the resources to grant whatever his eyes desired, and every pleasure of his heart.

i. "How many are there that have died of the wound in the eye!" (Trapp)

d. **For my heart rejoiced in all my labor**: We might say that the Preacher lived this period as a hedonist, but as an intelligent one. He looked for *legitimate* pleasures in life, such as the rightful pleasure one takes in the accomplishments of hard work (**my reward from all my labor**).

e. **Then I looked on all the works that my hands had done...indeed all was vanity and grasping for the wind**: Solomon examined his life lived for pleasure – even legitimate pleasures – and saw that it too was meaningless. **All was vanity**. There was no enduring, *eternal* sense of meaning to life lived for these earthly pleasures and accomplishments.

> i. "This is as modern as ennui [a feeling of dissatisfaction and uselessness] of every human soul which seeks knowledge, mirth, wealth, life – and forgets God." (Morgan)

B. The certainty and cruelty of death.

1. (12-17) Death makes equal the wise and the fool.

Then I turned myself to consider wisdom and madness and folly;
For what *can* the man *do* who succeeds the king?–
***Only* what he has already done.**
Then I saw that wisdom excels folly
As light excels darkness.
The wise man's eyes *are* in his head,
But the fool walks in darkness.
Yet I myself perceived
That the same event happens to them all.
So I said in my heart,
"As it happens to the fool,
It also happens to me,
And why was I then more wise?"
Then I said in my heart,
"This also *is* vanity."
For *there is* no more remembrance of the wise than of the fool forever,
Since all that now *is* will be forgotten in the days to come.
And how does a wise *man* die?
As the fool!

Therefore I hated life because the work that was done under the sun *was* distressing to me, for all *is* vanity and grasping for the wind.

a. **I turned myself to consider wisdom and madness and folly**: The Preacher continued to search after meaning and life, and followed the lines of **wisdom and madness and folly** further, unto their ending point.

b. **For what can the man do who succeeds the king**: Solomon here spoke of *himself* as the son of David (Ecclesiastes 1:1); yet he also spoke of his own successor (who turned out to be Rehoboam, 1 Kings 11:43). Of both, Solomon understood that the new king can do **only what he has already**

done. Even for a king, there is nothing new under the sun (Ecclesiastes 1:9).

c. **Wisdom excels folly.... Yet I myself perceived that the same event happens to them all**: The Preacher saw the meaninglessness of even wise living, pleasure, and accomplishment in a life lived *under the sun* – apart from the knowledge that eternity is real and God *matters*.

> i. No matter how wise one is or is not; how much they do or do not accomplish; or how much pleasure one has or does not have, **the same event happens to them all**: *they all die*. Given the Preacher's premise – that eternity and God do not matter – this is the only possible conclusion.

> ii. "Everything may tell us that wisdom is *not* on a par with folly, not goodness with evil; but no matter: if death is the end of the road, the contention that there is nothing to choose between them will get the last word." (Kidner)

d. **As it happens to the fool, it also happens to me, and why was I then more wise**: If death ends it all, then this life is robbed of true meaning. Even the good and great accomplishments of this world are unbelievably *temporary*, and therefore ultimately meaningless. The **wise man** dies just **as the fool**. Truly, the Preacher looked at this and said, **"This also is vanity."**

e. **Therefore I hated life...for all is vanity and grasping for the wind**: Given his premise of life *under the sun*, Solomon **hated life** because it was so meaningless (**vanity and grasping for the wind**).

> i. Adam Clarke says that **life** is more literally *lives*. "*The lives*, both of the *wise*, the *madman*, and the *fool*. Also all the *stages* of life, the *child*, the *man*, and the *sage*. There was nothing in it worth *pursuing*, no *period* worth *re-living* and no *hope* that if this were possible I could again be more successful."

> ii. **Therefore I hated life**: "If there is a lie at the centre of existence, and nonsense at the end of it, who has the heart to make anything of it?" (Kidner)

> iii. "He has no illusions, though by rights it is we who should have none – we who have heard from the secularists themselves that our very planet is dying." (Kidner)

2. (18-23) Death defeats all accomplishments.

Then I hated all my labor in which I had toiled under the sun, because I must leave it to the man who will come after me. And who knows whether he will be wise or a fool? Yet he will rule over all my labor in

which I toiled and in which I have shown myself wise under the sun. This also *is* vanity. Therefore I turned my heart and despaired of all the labor in which I had toiled under the sun. For there is a man whose labor *is* with wisdom, knowledge, and skill; yet he must leave his heritage to a man who has not labored for it. This also *is* vanity and a great evil. For what has man for all his labor, and for the striving of his heart with which he has toiled under the sun? For all his days *are* sorrowful, and his work burdensome; even in the night his heart takes no rest. This also is vanity.

a. **Then I hated all my labor...because I must leave it to a man who will come after me**: Not only did Solomon hate life under this thinking (Ecclesiastes 2:17), he also hated his very accomplishments, saying of them, **"This also is vanity."**

i. The idea that Solomon might leave all his work and material wealth to **a fool** seemed to trouble him. This concern was well founded, because after Solomon's death, Rehoboam turned out to be **a fool** in many ways (1 Kings 12, 1 Kings 14:21-31).

ii. "Alas! Solomon, the *wisest* of all men, made the *worst use* of his wisdom, had *seven hundred wives* and *three hundred concubines*, and yet left but *one son* behind him, to possess his *estates* and his *throne*, and that one was the silliest of fools!" (Clarke)

b. **There is a man whose labor is with wisdom, knowledge, and skill; yet he must leave his heritage to a man who has not labored for it**: Under his premise, death haunted Solomon. Not in the sense that he seemed afraid to die, but he despaired of how death (if that ends existence) makes all meaningless.

i. **I turned my heart and despaired of all the labor in which I had toiled under the sun**: "The only conclusion is that it is all useless. An abyss of despair results. He 'allowed [his] heart to despair' (as the Hebrew verb may be translated). This is one of the most moving points of the Old Testament, the antithesis of the New Testament's 'not in vain in the Lord' (1 Corinthians 15:58)." (Eaton)

c. **All his days are sorrowful, and his work burdensome; even in the night his heart takes no rest**: If death robs our work of meaning, then life is indeed **sorrowful**, work is **burdensome**, and there is no **rest** or relief from the despair of a meaningless life. Surely, this **also is vanity**.

i. Actually, it's worse than **vanity**. The Preacher also observed that in an **under the sun** world, this is **a great evil**.

ii. The Preacher hints at a vital question: *why does this bother us so?* If this is indeed man's lot and always has been; if every thought of an eternal meaning to life is a wish and a fantasy, *then why does that idea cause discontent in most everyone?* Man may *wish* he could fly like a bird, but there is little sense of meaninglessness in the heart of a man or woman because they cannot fly like a bird. This is because man was *not* designed to fly like a bird; but he *is* designed for eternity.

iii. "Incidentally, this bitter reaction is a witness to our ability to stand clear of our condition and to weigh it up. To be outraged at what is universal and unavoidable suggests something of a divine discontentment, and hint of what the great saying in 3:11 will call 'eternity' in man's mind." (Kidner)

C. How to live life "under the sun."

1. (24-25) Keeping a good attitude despite despair.

Nothing *is* better for a man *than* that he should eat and drink, and *that* his soul should enjoy good in his labor. This also, I saw, was from the hand of God. For who can eat, or who can have enjoyment, more than I?

a. **Nothing is better for a man than that he should eat and drink**: This thought is prominent in Ecclesiastes, being repeated some five times. It seems that the Preacher advised us how to make the best of a bad situation. If life really is as despairing and meaningless as he has shown it to be, then we should simply accept that true meaning is impossible to find, and simply find contentment in moderate and responsible pleasures.

i. This thinking is prominent in our day. Few people live for true, eternal meaning in their life; so they live with *under the sun* rules. They try to work hard, to enjoy life, to have fun, to be nice, to not get caught doing wrong, and they try not to hurt anybody.

ii. This thinking may work in making a bad situation better; but it gives no true *meaning* to life in light of eternity.

iii. "This may seem to savor of epicurism, as may also some following passages of this book. For which cause some of the old Jew doctors were once in a mind to hide this whole book out of the way, and not suffer the common sort to see it any more." (Trapp)

b. **This also, I saw, was from the hand of God**: We again see that the Preacher is no atheist; he certainly believes in God. But the God of the Preacher is not the God who matters and gives meaning to life as it is connected to eternity. The **God** of the Preacher simply teaches us to make the best of a bad situation.

i. "Everything is vanity. To live under the sun is to decide at last that the natural thing to do is to take what comes. Materialism necessarily becomes fatalism." (Morgan)

c. **For who can eat, or who can have enjoyment, more than I**: Given the Preacher's premise, his life should be the best in a meaningless world. He could enjoy this world of despair better than anyone else. Yet his life was almost infinitely poorer than the most humble life lived with true meaning.

2. (26) Perhaps the seeming injustice of this world may work to one's favor.

For *God* gives wisdom and knowledge and joy to a man who *is* good in His sight; but to the sinner He gives the work of gathering and collecting, that he may give to *him who is* good before God. This also *is* vanity and grasping for the wind.

a. **God gives wisdom and knowledge and joy to a man who is good**: Solomon reflected on how sometimes it seems that what the **sinner** has gathered and collected is given **to him who is good before God**. This might seem unjust, but even *under the sun*, sometimes injustice seems to work in one's favor.

i. "The fact that in the end the sinner's hoard will go to the righteous is only a crowning irony to what was in any case *vanity and a striving after the wind*." (Kidner)

b. **This also is vanity and grasping for the wind**: The Preacher knew that his seeming redistribution from God's hand was not enough to give true meaning to life lived *under the sun*.

Ecclesiastes 3 - The Reign of Time, A Glimmer of Hope

A. God and time.

1. (1-8) A time for every purpose.

To everything *there is* a season,
A time for every purpose under heaven:
A time to be born,
And a time to die;
A time to plant,
And a time to pluck *what is* planted;
A time to kill,
And a time to heal;
A time to break down,
And a time to build up;
A time to weep,
And a time to laugh;
A time to mourn,
And a time to dance;
A time to cast away stones,
And a time to gather stones;
A time to embrace,
And a time to refrain from embracing;
A time to gain,
And a time to lose;
A time to keep,
And a time to throw away;
A time to tear,
And a time to sew;
A time to keep silence,

And a time to speak;
A time to love,
And a time to hate;
A time of war,
And a time of peace.

a. **To everything there is a season, a time for every purpose under heaven**: The poetry of this list – describing the different seasons and facets of life – is beautiful. Yet it also casts a dark shadow because it reminds us of the inevitability of trouble and evil, and of the relentless monotony of life.

> i. "His ceaseless reiteration of the words, 'A time…a time…a time,' are intended to indicate his sense of the monotony of all things, rather than of their variety." (Morgan)

> ii. "The repetition of 'a time…, and a time…' begins to be oppressive. Whatever may be our skill and initiative, our real masters seem to be these inexorable seasons: not only those of the calendar, but that tide of events which moves us now to one kind of action which seems fitting, now to another which puts all into reverse." (Kidner)

b. **A time to be born, and a time to die…a time to break down, and a time to build up**: A bad facet answers each good facet. The Preacher understood that though there are good things in life, the bad things can't be escaped.

> i. "Birth and death, the boundaries of life under the sun, are mentioned first." (Wright)

> ii. **A time to kill**: Solomon did not tell us there was a time for murder. "Significantly, the Hebrew word used here for 'to kill,' is not the word reserved for murder in the sixth commandment, where premeditation seems to be in view." (Wright)

> iii. **A time to dance**: The English Puritan commentator John Trapp seemed to be wary of this **time to dance**. "Here is nothing for mixed immodest dancings…. Where there is dancing, there the devil is, saith a Father: and cannot men be merry unless they have the devil for their playfellow? Dancing, saith another, is a circle, whose centre is the devil, but busily blowing up the fire of lust, as in Herod, that old goat." (Trapp)

> iv. **A time to cast away stones**: In the ancient world they commonly scattered stones on an enemies' land to hinder farming.

> v. The poetic quality of the list shows that even the tragic, dark aspects of life can be artfully – and powerfully – presented.

vi. This list also shows us the need to take full advantage of the time God gives us (Ephesians 5:16, Colossians 4:15). "Many a man loseth his soul, as Saul did his kingdom, by not discerning his time. Esau came too late; so did the foolish virgins. If the gale of grace be over-past, the gate shut, the drawbridge taken up, there is no possibility of entrance." (Trapp)

2. (9-11) A glimmer of hope in seeing God as the master of time.

What profit has the worker from that in which he labors? I have seen the God-given task with which the sons of men are to be occupied. He has made everything beautiful in its time. Also He has put eternity in their hearts, except that no one can find out the work that God does from beginning to end.

a. **What profit has the worker from that in which he labors? I have seen the God-given task which the sons of men are to be occupied**: The Preacher asked the kind of question he had asked before; but this time he found an answer in **the God-given task** that God gives to man.

b. **He has made everything beautiful in its time**: This sense of balance considers the poetic list in the previous section. Solomon thought of the good and bad as they were described and understood that God **has made everything beautiful in its time**.

c. **Also He has put eternity in their hearts**: The Preacher understood that man has an awareness and a longing for the eternal, and that God has **put** this **in their hearts**. We can say that **eternity** is **in** our **hearts** because we are made in the image of an eternal God.

i. "God made man in his own image; and nothing more surely attests to the greatness of our origin that those faculties of the soul which are capable of yearning for, conceiving, and enjoying the Infinite, the Immortal, and the Divine.... Every appetite in nature and grace has its appropriate satisfaction." (Meyer)

ii. The well-known missionary and author Don Richardson used the phrase **eternity in their hearts** to describe the phenomenon of redemptive analogies in most all aboriginal cultures. Almost every culture has traditions, customs, or ways of thinking that reflect basic Biblical truth, and these can be used by missionaries to explain the gospel.

d. **Except that no one can find out the work that God does from beginning to end**: Though God has given man a longing for and awareness of eternity, God has not revealed very much about His eternal work. This keeps the yearning for **eternity** alive in the heart of man as a yet-to-be-fulfilled longing.

> i. "The Preacher's vast researches have found nothing in the finite earthly realm which can satisfy the human heart intellectually or practically.... This is the nearest he comes to Augustine's maxim: 'You have made us for yourself, and our hearts are restless until they can find peace in you.'" (Eaton)

3. (12-15) What the Preacher knows.

I know that nothing *is* better for them than to rejoice, and to do good in their lives, and also that every man should eat and drink and enjoy the good of all his labor—it *is* the gift of God.

I know that whatever God does,
It shall be forever.
Nothing can be added to it,
And nothing taken from it.
God does *it*, that men should fear before Him.
That which is has already been,
And what is to be has already been;
And God requires an account of what is past.

> a. **I know that nothing is better for them to rejoice, and to do good in their lives...and enjoy the good of all his labor—it is the gift of God**: In light of God's making **everything beautiful** and in His gift of **eternity in their hearts** – then it is wise to receive the good things of this life, and to receive them as **the gift of God**.

> > i. **I know**: This "holds out again hope of an enjoyable life from the hand of God...sees such a life as man's privilege." (Eaton)

> b. **I know that whatever God does, it shall be forever**: Here the Preacher escapes – ever so briefly – his *under the sun* thinking. It is not the mere mention of **God** that brings the escape; it is also the knowledge that God is eternal and that this *matters* to us (**God does it, that men should fear before Him**).

> > i. **I know**: This "shows the security of such a life is its divine guarantor... sees such a life...as God's purpose." (Eaton)

> > ii. Eaton sees three aspects of God's action highlighted in Ecclesiastes 3:14:

> > > • God's actions are permanent (**it shall be forever**).

> > > • God's actions are effective and complete (**nothing can be added to it**).

- God's actions are totally secure (**nothing taken from it**).

iii. "All this leads on the part of man to *fear*, not a craven terror in the face of the monstrous or the unknown, but rather the opposite, reverence and awesome regard for God." (Eaton)

c. **And God requires an account of what is past**: Again, this reflects a brief escape from *under the sun* thinking. If God judges the heart and deeds of man, then *everything* has meaning.

i. "God has no abortive enterprises or forgotten men. Once again Qoheleth has shown, in passing, that the despair he describes is not his own, and need not be ours." (Kidner)

B. Injustice is unanswered by death.

1. (16-17) The problem of injustice and an uneasy assurance of solving this problem.

Moreover I saw under the sun:
In **the place of judgment,**
Wickedness *was* **there;**
And *in* **the place of righteousness,**
Iniquity *was* **there.**
I said in my heart,
"God shall judge the righteous and the wicked,
For *there is* **a time there for every purpose and for every work."**

a. **I saw under the sun: in the place of judgment, wickedness was there**: Solomon looked at the world – the here and now world, apart from considering eternity – and saw that there was great evil and injustice. Instead of fair **judgment** he found **wickedness**; instead of **righteousness** he found **iniquity**.

i. "One of the greatest problems in understanding the total plan of God is that reward and punishment sometimes seem conspicuously absent." (Wright)

ii. This is a significant problem **under the sun**. If man does not have to reckon with eternity; if this life is all there is, then many of the wicked and evil people *win* and many good and righteous people *lose*. The idea of karma does not consistently work – at least not in this life.

b. **I said in my heart, "God shall judge the righteous and the wicked"**: The Preacher said – perhaps hoped – that he knew God would judge **the righteous and the wicked**, and not only in this life. Because **there is a time there for every purpose and for every work**, God will judge the deeds of man to see if it fit the proper **purpose** and **work**.

2. (18-21) The common fate of animals and humans *under the sun*.

I said in my heart, "Concerning the condition of the sons of men, God tests them, that they may see that they themselves are *like* animals." For what happens to the sons of men also happens to animals; one thing befalls them: as one dies, so dies the other. Surely, they all have one breath; man has no advantage over animals, for all *is* vanity. All go to one place: all are from the dust, and all return to dust. Who knows the spirit of the sons of men, which goes upward, and the spirit of the animal, which goes down to the earth?

a. **Concerning the condition of the sons of men...they themselves are like animals**: Solomon looked at life among both humans and animals, and also compared their deaths – doing so in *under the sun*, absent eternity terms. On this basis, he could say that there is little difference in the life and destiny between humans and animals.

i. **They themselves are like animals**: "The pronoun is repeated emphatically, 'that they themselves are [like] beasts, they in themselves.'" (Deane)

ii. "In their context these verses say that God makes all sensible people realize that they are as much subject to death as is the animal world." (Wright)

b. **As one dies, so dies the other**: The Preacher thought of an animal dying and its body decomposing. Then he thought that by all outward appearance, the same happens to a human body. Therefore, **they all have one breath; man has no advantage over animals, for all is vanity**.

i. "The distinction between man and beast in annulled by death; the former's boasted superiority, his power of conceiving and planning, his greatness, skill, strength, cunning, all come under the category of vanity, as they cannot ward off the inevitable blow." (Deane)

ii. This is no argument for the doctrine of annihilationism, the idea that the unrighteous dead simply cease to exist, either immediately or after some time of punishment. It is no argument for two reasons. First, Solomon spoke here as a man unconvinced of eternity and the meaning it brings to life. Second, we believe what 2 Timothy 1:10 says: that Jesus *brought life and immortality to light through the gospel.* The understanding of the afterlife is cloudy and uncertain in the Old Testament, but much clearer in the New Testament.

c. **Who knows the spirit of the sons of men, which goes upward, and the spirit of the animal, which goes down to the earth**: We sense that the Preacher *hoped* there was a different destiny between people and animals.

Yet in his *under the sun* thinking, there was no real reason to believe it – so, **"Who knows"**?

> i. "What is meant by 'upward' and 'downward' may be seen by reference to the gnome in Proverbs 15:24, 'To the wise the way of life goeth upward, that he may depart from Sheol beneath.'" (Deane)

> ii. "The Teacher is speaking phenomenologically, i.e., as things appear to the senses." (Wright)

3. (22) Finding peace *under the sun*.

So I perceived that nothing *is* better than that a man should rejoice in his own works, for that *is* his heritage. For who can bring him to see what will happen after him?

> a. **So I perceived**: It is true that Solomon **perceived** this, but he did so on the faulty assumptions of *under the sun* thinking.

> b. **Nothing is better than that a man should rejoice in his own works... who can bring him to see what will happen after him**: After briefly flirting with a confidence in eternity (Ecclesiastes 3:9-15), the Preacher has returned to his *under the sun* thinking. Under that premise, **nothing is better** than for a man to accomplish what he can in this world and try – the best he can – not to trouble himself about **what will happen after him**.

> > i. In his *under the sun* thinking, Solomon has an answer for the question, **"What will happen after him?"** The answer is, *nothing* – because death ends it all, and therefore ultimately his life has no more significance or meaning than the life of an animal.

Ecclesiastes 4 - Bittersweet Accomplishments

A. The tragedy of oppression.

1. (1) The comfortless oppression of man **under the sun**.

Then I returned and considered all the oppression that is done under the sun:
And look! The tears of the oppressed,
But they have no comforter—
On the side of their oppressors *there is* **power,**
But they have no comforter.

a. **I returned and considered all the oppression that is done under the sun**: After a brief flirtation with hope, the Preacher once again turned to despair at the end of Ecclesiastes 3 when he considered the problem of injustice. Continuing with that idea, he then **considered all the oppression that is done under the sun**.

i. "Compassion for the *oppressed* is common in the Old Testament." (Eaton)

- Oppression of people by a king (Proverbs 28:16).
- Oppression of a servant by his master (Deuteronomy 24:14).
- Oppression of the poor by the affluent (Proverbs 22:16).
- Oppression of the poor by the bureaucratic (Ecclesiastes 5:8).
- Oppression of the poor by other poor people (Proverbs 28:3).
- Oppression of the alien, the fatherless, and the widow (Jeremiah 7:6; Ezekiel 22:7; Zechariah 7:10).
- Oppression by charging high interest (Ezekiel 22:12, 29).
- Oppression by using false weights and measures (Hosea 12:7).

b. **The tears of the oppressed, but they have no comforter**: Solomon thought of the painful and tear-filled lives of the oppressed. In an **under**

the sun world – where this life is all there is, men and women give no account for their lives in a world to come – the **tears of the oppressed** are especially bitter and **they have no comforter**.

i. "Oh the tears for the oppressed; the tiny children; the terror-stricken fugitives from the Turk, the European trader, and the drunken tyrant of the home! Through all the centuries tears have flowed, enough to float a navy." (Meyer)

2. (2-3) Because of oppression and sadness, man is better off dead.

Therefore I praised the dead who were already dead,
More than the living who are still alive.
Yet, better than both *is he* who has never existed,
Who has not seen the evil work that is done under the sun.

a. **Therefore I praised the dead who were already dead**: The thought of both oppressors and their victims finding no justice in eternity was so bitter to the Preacher that he thought the dead fortunate. In an **under the sun** world, the dead do not have to think about such painful things.

i. Solomon could only praise the dead this way because at his time he had no certain knowledge of the world to come, and he wrote most of Ecclesiastes with an *under the sun* premise. If he knew and accepted what happened to the unrighteous dead, he would never say such a thing. "Men, like silly fishes, see one another caught and jerked out of the pond of life but they see not, alas! the fire and the pan into which they are cast that die in their sins." (Trapp)

ii. **The dead who were already dead** is an interesting phrase. It implies that there are **the dead** who are not yet **dead** – the living dead, so to speak. They walk this earth and have biological life, but their spirit and soul seem dead.

b. **Better than both is he who has never existed, who has not seen the evil work that is done under the sun**: Solomon took the idea of praising the dead even further, to where he no praised **he who has never existed**. Even the dead were once alive and had to see **the evil work that is done under the sun**.

i. "There is nothing sadder in the whole book than the wistful glance in verses 2 and 3 at the dead and the unborn, who are spared the sight of so much anguish." (Kidner)

ii. Jesus Himself said there was one man for whom it would have been better if he had never been born: Judas (Matthew 26:24).

iii. The Preacher's great despair over the injustice of oppression in an **under the sun** premise shows the moral necessity of an afterlife and a coming judgment. Jesus told us that it is those who oppress and misuse their power who will ultimately endure punishment, not their victims (Matthew 18:6-7).

B. Bittersweet accomplishments.

1. (4-6) Success often gains the envy of one's neighbor.

Again, I saw that for all toil and every skillful work a man is envied by his neighbor. This also *is* vanity and grasping for the wind.

The fool folds his hands
And consumes his own flesh.
Better a handful *with* quietness
Than both hands full, *together with* toil and grasping for the wind.

a. **For all toil and every skillful work a man is envied by his neighbor**: The Preacher thought of those who gain success through **toil** and **skillful work** – and how it simply brought envy and sometimes hatred from others. This common jealousy of success made life seem like **vanity and grasping for the wind**.

i. "For if a man act uprightly and properly in the world, he soon becomes the object of his neighbour's envy and calumny too. Therefore the encouragement to do good, to act an upright part, is very little. This constitutes a part of the *vain* and *empty* system of human life." (Clarke)

b. **The fool folds his hands and consumes his own flesh**: Solomon here answered the tendency for those jealous of the success of others to be lazy. Like **fools**, they fold their hands and do nothing – and so waste away. Yet it wasn't the success of their neighbor that made them waste away; the foolish, lazy man **consumes his own flesh**.

i. **Consumes his own flesh**: "This expression is really equivalent to 'destroys himself,' 'brings ruin upon himself.'" (Deane) A similar thought from a different perspective is found in Psalm 27:2.

c. **Better a handful with quietness than both hands full, together with toil and grasping for the wind**: The Preacher reflects on the value of *contentment*. It is better to have less and be content (**with quietness**) than to have more and constantly be grasping for further success.

i. Solomon weaved some fascinating themes together.

- Hard work and success are good and not to be envied.

- Laziness is wrong and destructive.

- Yet even the one with full hands must learn contentment.

2. (7-8) What good is your success if you can't pass it on?

Then I returned, and I saw vanity under the sun:
There is one alone, without companion:
He has neither son nor brother.
Yet *there is* no end to all his labors,
Nor is his eye satisfied with riches.
But he never asks,
"For whom do I toil and deprive myself of good?"
This also *is* vanity and a grave misfortune.

a. **There is one alone, without companion**: Solomon thought of a man alone, without family or close friends.

b. **Yet there is no end to all his labors, nor is his eye satisfied with riches**: The man in Solomon's thinking works hard and wants to gain more and more.

c. **But he never asks, "For whom do I toil and deprive myself of good"**: The Preacher thought this unexamined life of hard work and success – without family and friends to share in it all – is **vanity and a grave misfortune**.

i. The Preacher was entirely correct from an *under the sun* perspective. Under that premise, there is no such thing as an eternal accomplishment and one does not even have the *potential* satisfaction of passing one's accomplishments on to another.

ii. "This picture of lonely, pointless busyness, equally with that of jealous rivalry in verse 4, checks any excessive claims we might wish to make for the blessings of hard work." (Kidner)

3. (9-12) Without a friend, accomplishments are vain.

Two *are* better than one,
Because they have a good reward for their labor.
For if they fall, one will lift up his companion.
But woe to him *who is* alone when he falls,
For *he has* no one to help him up.
Again, if two lie down together, they will keep warm;
But how can one be warm *alone?*
Though one may be overpowered by another, two can withstand him.
And a threefold cord is not quickly broken.

a. **Two are better than one**: In the previous section Solomon thought how even in an *under the sun* world, living alone made life worse. He continues to develop the same idea, noting that **two are better than one** and will begin to state the reasons why this is true.

> i. "Having looked at the poverty of the 'loner', whatever his outward success, we now reflect on something better; and *better* will be a key word here." (Kidner)

b. **Because they have a good reward for their labor**: In a good partnership, two can accomplish more than each one individually. The sum will be greater than the parts.

c. **If they fall, one will lift us his companion**: When two work and live together they can help each other in difficult times – **but woe to him who is alone when he falls, for he has no one to help him up**. The Preacher understood that everybody *needs* help, and it is a blessing both to give and to receive help.

d. **If two lie down together, they will keep warm; but how can one be warm alone**: When two work and live together they can bring comfort to the lives of each other.

e. **Though one may be overpowered by another, two can withstand him**: When two work and live together, they can bring security and safety to each other. To use a familiar phrase, they can "watch the back" of one another.

> i. These four verses show us the great value of human relationships, that **two are better than one**. Living and working together is a great advantage to living and working alone, and adds these four things to life:
>
> - Productivity (**they have a good reward for their labor**).
> - Help in need (**If they fall, one will lift up his companion**).
> - Comfort in life (**they will keep warm**).
> - Safety and security (**two can withstand**).

f. **A threefold cord is not quickly broken**: The Preacher gives a fascinating final line to this section dealing with the goodness of companionship. We might have excepted that he would praise the strength of a *twofold* cord; instead he noted that **a threefold is not quickly broken**. It is commonly understood that the *third* cord is God Himself, and that a relationship intertwined with God is **a threefold cord** that **is not quickly broken**.

> i. "The strength of the three-ply cord was proverbial in the ancient world." (Eaton)

ii. This is commonly applied – and well applied – to the idea of recognizing and embracing God in the marriage relationship. Yet it is possible that, in the context of marriage and family, Solomon had *children* in mind with the picture of **a threefold cord**.

4. (13-16) The vanity of fame and its short life.

Better a poor and wise youth
Than an old and foolish king who will be admonished no more.
For he comes out of prison to be king,
Although he was born poor in his kingdom.
I saw all the living who walk under the sun;
They were with the second youth who stands in his place.
There was **no end of all the people over whom he was made king;**
Yet those who come afterward will not rejoice in him.
Surely this also *is* **vanity and grasping for the wind.**

a. **Better a poor and wise youth than an old and foolish king who will be admonished no more**: The Preacher begins this section with a proverb, observing that it is better to be poor and wise (and young!) than to be old, foolish and have great wealth and status.

b. **He comes out of prison to be king**: Solomon thought of a second young man, who rose out of misfortune and obscurity to achieve great wealth, status, and fame (**there was no end of all the people over whom he was made king**).

c. **Yet those who come afterward will not rejoice in him**: As Solomon thought of this young man who achieved much and became famous, he understood that the fame would be short-lived. Even if it lasted his entire lifetime (which would be rare and remarkable), it would not live on much beyond his own life. With his *under the sun* premise, this thought brought the familiar conclusion to the Preacher: **Surely this also is vanity and grasping for the wind**.

i. "He has reached a pinnacle of human glory, only to be stranded there. It is yet another of our human anticlimaxes and ultimately empty achievements." (Kidner)

Ecclesiastes 5 - Reverent Worship

A. Worshipping God reverently.

1. (1-3) Come to the house of God more to hear and to obey than to speak.

Walk prudently when you go to the house of God; and draw near to hear rather than to give the sacrifice of fools, for they do not know that they do evil.

Do not be rash with your mouth,
And let not your heart utter anything hastily before God.
For God *is* in heaven, and you on earth;
Therefore let your words be few.
For a dream comes through much activity,
And a fool's voice *is known* by *his* many words.

a. **Walk prudently when you go to the house of God**: Solomon here brings good advice that does not contradict his *under the sun* premise. Even apart from eternity, it would be wise to honor God and **walk prudently when you go to the house of God** for the sake of this life alone.

b. **Walk prudently when you go to the house of God**: The Preacher will explain more of what this means in the coming lines. Yet generally we can say that it means to show care and think about consequences when we come to meet God.

i. "Fruitful and acceptable worship begins before it begins." (Maclaren)

c. **Draw near to hear rather than to give the sacrifice of fools**: The **sacrifice of fools** is the hasty speech mentioned in the next lines. Solomon counsels us the come to the house of God **to hear** more than to speak without thinking.

i. **To hear**: "Has the double force in Hebrew which it sometimes has in English: to pay attention and to obey. So this saying is close to the famous words of Samuel, 'to obey (literally to listen) is better than sacrifice' (1 Samuel 15:22)." (Kidner)

ii. "They who fall into the faults condemned are 'fools.' If that class includes all who mar their worship by such errors, the church which holds them had need to be of huge dimensions; for the faults held up in these ancient words flourish in full luxuriance to-day." (Maclaren)

iii. **Sacrifice**: "The *zebah* was an offering killed in sacrifice and then used for a meal, in contrast to the whole burnt-offering (*ola*) which was totally consumed in sacrifice. As Delitzsch points out, it is the *zebah* which could degenerate into thoughtless festivity, or worse." (Eaton)

d. **Do not be rash with your mouth...for God is in heaven, and you on earth; therefore let your words be few**: Solomon rightly described the human tendency to speak without thinking before God and others. Even with an *under the sun* premise, it is foolish to speak too much and hear too little in God's presence.

i. "When we come before God, our minds are full of our own business rather than with the worship of God. When we talk too much, we usually talk like fools. This can be especially bad in the house of God." (Wright)

ii. The priests of Baal prayed hard and long on Mount Carmel; Elijah prayed short and sweet, and full of faith to the living God. God heard and beautifully answered Elijah's prayer (1 Kings 18).

iii. J. Edwin Orr used to advise brief, earnest prayers, especially in prayer meetings. He said that when one prays in a meeting, for his first three minutes everyone prays *with* him. Should he continue a second three minutes, everyone prays *for* him. Should he continue for a third three minutes, the others start to pray *against* him.

iv. "For as it is not the loudness of a preacher's voice, but the weight and holiness of his matter, and the spirit of the preacher, that moves a wise and intelligent hearer, so it is not the labour of the lips, but the travail of the heart that prevails with God." (Trapp)

e. **A dream comes through much activity, and a fool's voice is known by his many words**: The thought in this line is probably well represented by the Living Bible: "Just as being too busy gives you nightmares, so being a fool makes you a blabbermouth."

i. "As personal and business cares produce dreams, which are unsubstantial things; so many words produce foolish and empty prayers." (Wright)

2. (4-7) Keep your vows and fear God.

When you make a vow to God, do not delay to pay it;
For *He has* no pleasure in fools.
Pay what you have vowed—
Better not to vow than to vow and not pay.

Do not let your mouth cause your flesh to sin, nor say before the messenger *of God* that it *was* an error. Why should God be angry at your excuse and destroy the work of your hands? For in the multitude of dreams and many words *there is* also vanity. But fear God.

a. **When you make a vow to God, do not delay to pay it**: Even with an *under the sun* premise, it is both honorable and wise to honor God by keeping one's word to Him. It would be **better not to vow than to vow and not pay**.

i. "God does not take broken vows lightly. A broken vow may incur his judgment upon our endeavours. One who 'swears to his own hurt and does not change' pleases God (Psalm 15:4)." (Eaton)

ii. A commonly overlooked and unappreciated sin among God's people is the sin of *broken vows* - promising things to God and failing to live up to the vow. Those who honor God:

- Will not be quick to make vows to God.
- Will be serious about fulfilling vows made.
- Will regard broken vows as sins to confessed and to be repented of.

b. **Do not let your mouth cause your flesh to sin, nor say...that it was an error**: The Preacher rightly observed that it was important for God's people to regard their *failure* to keep vows as a serious matter, and that great effort should be put into keeping vows and not regarding the failure to keep them as simply an "**error**."

i. **Say before the messenger of God that it was an error**: "Hebrew draws no distinction between *messenger* and *angel*, so several interpretations are open to us here." (Eaton)

c. **Fear God**: Solomon counseled reverence and honor towards God, but in his *under the sun* perspective the value is found in the here-and-now, not unto eternity.

i. "Most certainly, he that fears God need fear nothing else. Well may an upright soul say to *Satan* himself, I fear God; and because I fear *him*, l do not fear *thee*." (Clarke)

B. The vanity of wealth and materialism.

1. (8-9) The enduring fact of oppression and injustice.

If you see the oppression of the poor, and the violent perversion of justice and righteousness in a province, do not marvel at the matter; for high official watches over high official, and higher officials are over them. Moreover the profit of the land is for all; *even* **the king is served from the field.**

a. **If you see the oppression of the poor, and the violent perversion of justice...do not marvel at the matter**: The Preacher spoke realistically about life *under the sun*. There is much **oppression** and **perversion of justice**. It should surprise no one.

i. "For all his hatred of injustice, Qoheleth pins no hopes on utopian schemes or on revolution. He knows what is in man." (Kidner)

b. **For high official watches over high official, and higher officials are over them**: Solomon was especially aware of how bureaucracies can bring oppression.

c. **Moreover the profit of the land is for all; even the king is served from the field**: Even with a complex (and possibly corrupt) bureaucracy, *everyone* depends on what comes from the farmer's field – **even the king**. The Preacher seemed to delight in these ironies of life.

i. "Without the field he cannot have supplies for his own house; and, unless *agriculture* flourish, the necessary expenses of the state cannot be defrayed. Thus, God joins the *head* and *feet* together; for while the peasant is protected by the king as executor of the laws, the king himself is dependent on the peasant; as the wealth of the nation is the fruit of the labourer's toil."

ii. "Some read it thus: *Rex agro servit*, The king is a servant to the field." (Trapp)

2. (10-12) Dissatisfaction in the accumulation of wealth.

He who loves silver will not be satisfied with silver;
Nor he who loves abundance, with increase.
This also *is* **vanity.**
When goods increase,
They increase who eat them;
So what profit have the owners
Except to see *them* **with their eyes?**
The sleep of a laboring man *is* **sweet,**

Whether he eats little or much;
But the abundance of the rich will not permit him to sleep.

a. **He who loves silver will not be satisfied with silver**: Of all people, Solomon knew that the gathering of riches did not satisfy. He knew, **this also is vanity**.

i. "If anything is worse than the addiction money brings, it is the emptiness it leaves. Man, with eternity in his heart, needs better nourishment than this." (Kidner)

b. **When goods increase, they increase who eat them; so what profit have the owners**: Solomon knew that as one's net worth increased, so did one's expenses – *and* the expectation of others.

i. "Servants, friends, flatterers, trencher-men, pensioners, and other hangbys that will flock to a rich man, as crows do to a dead carcase, not to defend, but to devour it." (Trapp)

c. **The sleep of the laboring man is sweet...the abundance of the rich will not permit him to sleep**: Solomon indulged an envy of the **laboring man**, who has so much less to worry about. The **rich** man has greater worries and less **sleep**.

i. We may suppose that Solomon found little sympathy from **the laboring man**.

3. (13-17) The uncertainty of wealth.

There is a severe evil *which* I have seen under the sun:
Riches kept for their owner to his hurt.
But those riches perish through misfortune;
When he begets a son, *there is* nothing in his hand.
As he came from his mother's womb, naked shall he return,
To go as he came;
And he shall take nothing from his labor
Which he may carry away in his hand.
And this also *is* a severe evil—
Just exactly as he came, so shall he go.
And what profit has he who has labored for the wind?
All his days he also eats in darkness,
And *he has* much sorrow and sickness and anger.

a. **A severe evil...riches kept for their owner to his hurt**: Solomon then observed that wealth does not *bless* the life of every wealthy person. Especially those who keep their riches with an ungenerous, clenched fist, they are **riches kept for their owner to his hurt**.

i. "Rather, *preserved by the possessor*, hoarded and guarded, only to bring their lord added grief when by some reverse of fortune he loses them, as explained in what follows." (Deane)

b. **But those riches perish through misfortune...he shall take nothing from his labor**: This shows further the foolishness of holding on to wealth in an ungenerous way. Wealth can disappear suddenly **through misfortune**; yet we lose all wealth in death. Solomon knew that despite the burial wishes and customs of the pharaohs, one cannot take their with wealth with them after death.

i. "The riches were suddenly and catastrophically lost, whether in foolish gambling, in a misguided venture, or in a sudden reversal of circumstances." (Eaton)

c. **Just exactly as he came, so shall he go**: Solomon understood that great wealth ultimately means nothing *under the sun*. Man comes with nothing into the world and leaves the same way.

i. The New Testament gives a more hopeful picture, taking us beyond the Preacher's *under the sun* premise and telling us that we can lay up treasure in heaven. You can't take your wealth with you when you die; but you can send it on ahead by generous giving to God's work.

d. **All his days he also eats in darkness, and he has much sorrow and sickness and anger**: With a sympathetic touch, Solomon tells us the loneliness, **sorrow**, and **anger** there is even for the very wealthy.

4. (18-20) Making the best of a bad situation *under the sun*.

Here is what I have seen: *It is* **good and fitting** *for one* **to eat and drink, and to enjoy the good of all his labor in which he toils under the sun all the days of his life which God gives him; for it** *is* **his heritage. As for every man to whom God has given riches and wealth, and given him power to eat of it, to receive his heritage and rejoice in his labor—this** *is* **the gift of God. For he will not dwell unduly on the days of his life, because God keeps** *him* **busy with the joy of his heart.**

a. **It is good and fitting for one to eat and drink, and enjoy the good of all his labor in which he toils under the sun**: We sense that Solomon – still very much with the premise of *under the sun* – simply hoped to make the best of a bad situation.

b. **As for every man to whom God has given riches and wealth...this is the gift of God**: Though the Preacher knew that riches did not bring true meaning to life, he was no fool. He understood that it was better to have wealth than to not have it, and *under the sun*, one should enjoy both wealth and the capacity to enjoy it as **the gift of God**.

i. "Indeed, the very care of wealth becomes a reason for restlessness. In view of all these things there is but one attitude, which the preacher advises: Do not hoard anything, but enjoy it." (Morgan)

c. **For he will not dwell unduly on the days of his life, because God keeps him busy with the joy of his heart**: This was Solomon's counsel to the wealthy man who finds no ultimate meaning *under the sun*. Simply, *try not to think about it and keep yourself busy.*

Ecclesiastes 6 - Wealth Can't Satisfy

A. The weakness of wealth

1. (1-2) Others can take one's wealth.

There is an evil which I have seen under the sun, and it *is* common among men: A man to whom God has given riches and wealth and honor, so that he lacks nothing for himself of all he desires; yet God does not give him power to eat of it, but a foreigner consumes it. This *is* vanity, and it *is* an evil affliction.

> a. **There is an evil which I have seen under the sun**: The Preacher still speaks from his **under the sun** premise.

> b. **A man to whom God has given riches and wealth and honor, so that he lacks nothing...yet God does not give him power to eat of it, but a foreigner consumes it**: Solomon saw the tragedy of those who are given great gifts from God – yet they do not have the opportunity to enjoy what God gives. Solomon understood this to be **vanity** and **an evil affliction**.

2. (3-6) The meaninglessness of life that does not go beyond death.

If a man begets a hundred *children* and lives many years, so that the days of his years are many, but his soul is not satisfied with goodness, or indeed he has no burial, I say *that* a stillborn child *is* better than he—for it comes in vanity and departs in darkness, and its name is covered with darkness. Though it has not seen the sun or known *anything*, this has more rest than that man, even if he lives a thousand years twice—but has not seen goodness. Do not all go to one place?

> a. **If a man begets a hundred children and lives many years...but his soul is not satisfied with goodness**: The Preacher knew that a man could have all the outward signs of a good life – but still not be **satisfied with goodness**.

i. "One could have the things men dream of – which in Old Testament terms meant children by the score, and years of life by the thousand – and still depart unnoticed, unlamented, and unfulfilled." (Kidner)

ii. "Like the Mosaic law (*cf.* Galatians 3:22), the Preacher is slamming every door except the door of faith." (Eaton)

b. **I say that a stillborn child is better than he**: This is a bitter statement, the kind we might expect from one who had suffered like Job (Job 3). Yet Solomon – with all his blessings and advantages – felt and knew the same despair of life as Job had. Life seemed so meaningless that he felt it would be better if he had never been born.

i. "To die unburied was the mark of a despised and unmourned end. Better to miscarry at birth than to miscarry throughout life." (Eaton)

c. **Though it has not seen the sun or known anything, this has more rest than that man, even if he lives a thousand years twice – but has not seen goodness**: In Solomon's mind, the stillborn child – tragic as it is – is better off than the man who knows the crushing disappointment of the realization of meaninglessness, **even if he lives a thousand years**.

d. **Do not all go to one place**: Solomon writes with his *under the sun* perspective, and shares much of the Old Testament uncertainty about the afterlife.

B. What good is it all?

1. (7-9) Suffering under dissatisfaction.

All the labor of man *is* for his mouth,
And yet the soul is not satisfied.
For what more has the wise *man* than the fool?
What does the poor man have,
Who knows *how* to walk before the living?
Better *is* the sight of the eyes than the wandering of desire.
This also *is* vanity and grasping for the wind.

a. **All the labor of man is for his mouth, and yet the soul is not satisfied**: Man works for the very bread he eats, yet it does not satisfy his soul. Solomon sensed what Moses had already said and Jesus later repeated: *Man does not live by bread alone* (Deuteronomy 8:3, Matthew 3:4).

b. **What more has the wise man than the fool**: Wisdom itself can't fill a hungry man's stomach. For all the superiority of the **wise man** compared to the fool, they both get hungry. Being **wise** isn't as much of an advantage as commonly thought.

i. "The necessaries of life are the same to both, and their *condition* in life is nearly similar; liable to the same diseases, dissolution, and death." (Clarke)

c. **Better is the sight of the eyes than the wandering of desire**: The Preacher knew that in a world of such uncertainty and absence of meaning, that what one can actually see is always better than what one merely desires.

2. (10-12) The futility of feeling that nothing can make it better.

Whatever one is, he has been named already,
For it is known that he *is* man;
And he cannot contend with Him who is mightier than he.
Since there are many things that increase vanity,
How *is* man the better?

For who knows what *is* good for man in life, all the days of his vain life which he passes like a shadow? Who can tell a man what will happen after him under the sun?

a. **Whatever one is, he has been named already**: This is a fatalistic view of God's sovereignty. The idea is that God is completely in control, and **whatever one is**, it is because the all-powerful God has **named** it already.

i. "Since God is supreme, he has surely predestined everything and has made man too weak to resist. Reasoning, complaining, and arguing bring no answer and lead to further frustration." (Wright)

b. **He cannot contend with Him who is mightier than he**: Solomon's great frustration is rooted in the understanding that man is man, God is God, and man can never successfully **contend with Him who is mightier than he**.

i. Many today refuse to know what the Preacher knew. They believe that when they face God (abandoning Solomon's *under the sun* premise) they will in fact **contend with Him**, and tell God a thing or two. Such are seriously and sadly deluded.

ii. "God will have the better of those that contend with him: and his own reason will tell him that it is not fit that God should cast down the bucklers first: and that the deeper a man wades, the more he shall be wet." (Trapp)

c. **Since there are many things that increase vanity, how is man the better**: The Preacher felt that life was a game that could not be won. There were too many **things that increase vanity** that ultimately man would become **no better**.

i. "Evidently the thought of the preacher is that the more a man possesses under the sun, the more profoundly conscious does he become of the vanity and vexation of it all." (Morgan)

d. **For who knows what is good for man in life**: We often *think* we know what is **good** for us; but do we really? In the course of a life, which is better: Wealth or poverty? Health or sickness? Fame or obscurity? Many who have what is commonly thought of as **good** are not the better for it.

e. **All the days of his vain life which he passes like a shadow? Who can tell a man what will happen after him under the sun**: Solomon looked to life and it seemed **vain** and a **shadow**. He looked to death and saw only darkness and uncertainty. To this point there is little relief from the tragedy of meaninglessness of life (and death) *under the sun.*

i. "So the chapter will wind its way down to a depressing and uncertain finish, well suited to the state of man on his own." (Kidner)

ii. We can explain Solomon's lack of knowledge of the afterlife by understanding the principle of 2 Timothy 2:10: that Jesus Christ *brought life and immortality to light through the gospel.* The understanding of immortality was at best cloudy in the Old Testament but is much clearer in the New Testament. For example, we can say that Jesus knew fully what He was talking about when He described hell and judgment (such as in Matthew 25:41-46). We therefore rely on the *New* Testament for our understanding of the afterlife, much more than the *Old.*

iii. We also understand that this does not in any way take away from the truth of the Bible and the Book of Ecclesiastes. What is true is that Solomon actually wrote this and actually believed it (with his *under the sun* premise); the truth of the statement itself must be evaluated according to the rest of the Bible.

Ecclesiastes 7 - Trying to Find a Better Way

A. Looking at life through better and worse.

1. (1-4) Better in life and death.

**A good name *is* better than precious ointment,
And the day of death than the day of one's birth;
Better to go to the house of mourning
Than to go to the house of feasting,
For that *is* the end of all men;
And the living will take *it* to heart.
Sorrow *is* better than laughter,
For by a sad countenance the heart is made better.
The heart of the wise *is* in the house of mourning,
But the heart of fools *is* in the house of mirth.**

a. **A good name is better than precious ointment, and the day of death better than the day of one's birth**: At the end of Ecclesiastes 6, the Preacher was in a mournful, discouraged mood as he considered the meaninglessness of life in a world without eternity and accountability in the world beyond. He continued that tone by coupling an obvious truth (**a good name is better than precious ointment**) with a more startling statement (**the day of death better than the day of one's birth**).

i. This comes from the deep and pained sense of meaninglessness that the Preacher suffered under. It made him feel that **death** was better than life.

ii. "Nothing in the first half of verse 1 prepares us for the body-blow of the second half... Instead of reflecting and arguing, he will bombard us with proverbs, with their strong impact and varied angles of attack." (Kidner)

iii. Even **the day of one's birth** is ominous, despite all the hopes and potential in a baby's birth. Children come into the world uttering the *human sound* – a scream. "Before ever a child speak, he prophesies, by his tears, of his ensuing sorrows." (Trapp)

iv. From a New Testament perspective, we have mixed feelings about the Preacher's outburst, "**The day of death better than the day of one's birth**." On the one hand, **the day of death** *is* glorious for the believer – our battle is over, our sorrow is over, our uncertainty is over – and all things are new. On the other hand, we rejoice in the meaning God has given us with this life on earth. We agree with the Apostle Paul in Philippians 1:23: *For I am hard pressed between the two, having a desire to depart and be with Christ, which is far better.*

v. "Death is the end of dying. On the day of the believer's death dying is for ever done with. The saints who are with God shall never die any more. Life is wrestling, struggling; but death is the end of conflict: it is rest-victory." (Spurgeon)

vi. "Hence all the ancient fathers called those days wherein the martyrs suffered their birthdays, because they began to live indeed." (Trapp)

vii. "Consider it spiritually, and, dear brethren, what is a good name? A good name is a name that is written in the Lamb's book of life, and that is better than the sweetest of all ointments." (Spurgeon)

b. **Better to go to the house of mourning than to the house of feasting**: Solomon knew our tendency to simply *ignore* or *wish away* death. It is better to be squarely confronted with the reality of death, and **the house of mourning** is a fine place to **take it to heart**.

i. It seems that the Preacher has rejected his previous hope of finding the meaning of life in pleasure, accomplishment, and wisdom. Now there is only death, and one should not ignore it. *So teach us to number our days, that we may gain a heart of wisdom.* (Psalm 90:12)

ii. "Some of the old Romish monks always read their Bibles with a candle stuck in a skull. The light from a death's head may be an awful one, but it is a very profitable one." (Spurgeon)

c. **Sorrow is better than laughter**: The Preacher goes against all intuition; who among us would say this? Yet he is determined to sweep away our illusions and wishes about the nature of life in his *under the sun* premise.

i. Rejecting Solomon's general premise, we do not believe that **sorrow is** *always* **better than laughter**. We do not reject it because we prefer an illusion or a wish; we do it out of firm confidence in a God to whom we answer in eternity, and who has promised to reward good and punish evil there. Even so – there *is* often more wisdom **in the house of mourning** than **in the house of mirth**.

2. (5-9) Better in wisdom and folly.

It is **better to hear the rebuke of the wise**
Than for a man to hear the song of fools.
For like the crackling of thorns under a pot,
So *is* **the laughter of the fool.**
This also is vanity.
Surely oppression destroys a wise *man's* **reason,**
And a bribe debases the heart.
The end of a thing *is* **better than its beginning;**
The patient in spirit *is* **better than the proud in spirit.**
Do not hasten in your spirit to be angry,
For anger rests in the bosom of fools.

a. **It is better to hear the rebuke of the wise than for a man to hear the song of fools**: The Preacher continues his previous thought, that man finds wisdom in adversity and suffering than in ease and comfort. The **laughter of the fool** is nothing more than a momentary sound, leaving nothing of substance behind.

i. "The pun 'Like the sound of *sirim* (thorns) under the *sir* (pot, cauldron)' is caught by Moffatt's *Like nettles crackling under kettles*. Thorns were a rapidly burning, easily extinguishable fuel in the ancient world." (Eaton)

ii. "They make a great noise, a great blaze; and are extinguished in a few moments. Such indeed, comparatively, are the joys of life; they are noisy, flashy, and transitory." (Clarke)

iii. "Their laughter is also fitly compared to thorns, because it chokes good motions, scratcheth the conscience, harbours the vermin of base and baggage lusts." (Trapp)

b. **Surely oppression destroys a wise man's reason**: For all of Solomon's praise of the instructive role of adversity, he also understood that suffering also had its limit. It could destroy **a wise man's reason**.

c. **Do not hasten your spirit to be angry**: After two proverbs celebrating patience, the Preacher warns us against impatience leading to anger. Living with an *under the sun* premise may easily make a person impatient and then angry, and **anger rests in the bosom of fools**.

3. (10-12) Wisdom gives perspective.

Do not say,
"Why were the former days better than these?"
For you do not inquire wisely concerning this.
Wisdom *is* good with an inheritance,
And profitable to those who see the sun.
For wisdom *is* a defense *as* money *is* a defense,
But the excellence of knowledge *is that* wisdom gives life to those who have it.

a. **Do not say, "Why were the former days better than these"**: Solomon understood our tendency to romanticize the past and think that it was better than our current time. He cautioned against it, knowing that the meaninglessness of life with his *under the sun* premise is not a new phenomenon.

i. "The clear-eyed Qoheleth is the last person to be impressed by this golden haze around the past: he has already declared that one age is very much like another. 'What has been is what will be...and there is nothing new under the sun' (Ecclesiastes 1:9)." (Kidner)

ii. "Even Christians sometimes overestimate the early church, the Reformation, or periods of revival. Wise people certainly learn from the past, but they live in the present with all its opportunities." (Wright)

iii. "In former days men were wicked as they are now, and religion was unfashionable: God also is the same *now* as he was *then*; as just, as merciful, as ready to help: and there is no depravity in the age that will excuse your crimes, your follies, and your carelessness." (Clarke)

b. **Wisdom is good with an inheritance, and profitable to those who see the sun**: With the Preacher's premise, the best kind of life is found with wisdom and money (**an inheritance**). This **wisdom** – called also **excellence of knowledge** – gives whatever life can be had in an *under the sun* world.

4. (13-14) Wisdom in considering God.

Consider the work of God;
For who can make straight what He has made crooked?
In the day of prosperity be joyful,
But in the day of adversity consider:
Surely God has appointed the one as well as the other,
So that man can find out nothing *that will come* after him.

a. **Consider the work of God; for who can make straight what He has made crooked**: Understanding the relative place of man to God is important in peaceful acceptance with life *under the sun*. From the Preacher's perspective, this has the sense of fatalism.

i. "There is no standing before a lion, no hoisting up a sail in a tempest, no contending with the Almighty." (Trapp)

b. **In the day of prosperity be joyful, but in the day of adversity consider**: Solomon counsels us how to take the good and the bad of life into perspective. "Take what life gives you and get along the best you can."

c. **Surely God has appointed the one as well as the other, so that man can find out nothing that will come after him**: The Preacher here drifts again toward despair. Considering God's control of all things leads him to believe that the system is set so that we can know nothing of what is beyond us, of what **will come after him**.

B. Living a better life under the sun.

1. (15-18) Dangers along the way.

I have seen everything in my days of vanity:
There is a just *man* who perishes in his righteousness,
And there is a wicked *man* who prolongs *life* in his wickedness.
Do not be overly righteous,
Nor be overly wise:
Why should you destroy yourself?
Do not be overly wicked,
Nor be foolish:
Why should you die before your time?
***It is* good that you grasp this,**
And also not remove your hand from the other;
For he who fears God will escape them all.

a. **I have seen everything in my days of vanity**: Solomon complained that in his meaningless life he has seen the good suffer (**a just man who perishes in his righteousness**) and the wicked prosper (**prolongs his life in his wickedness**). Solomon mourns, *it isn't fair*.

i. "The first man that died, died for religion. How early did martyrdom come into the world!" (Trapp)

b. **Do not be overly righteous, nor be overly wise...do not be overly wicked, nor be foolish**: In light of the apparent **vanity** of life, Solomon here recommended a *balanced* approach to living. Be **righteous**, but not too much; be **wise**, but not too much; be **wicked**, but not too much; be **foolish**, but not too much.

i. "Righteousness does not always pay. Wickedness sometimes does. Therefore morality is to be a thing of calculation." (Morgan)

ii. This is a common approach to life, thinking that everything is good in moderation. This has some truth to it but does not define a wise or good life. We should remember that both Jesus and Paul (as well as many others) were not considered balanced individuals in their day. Their understanding of eternity and accountability made them – in the view of many – *unbalanced*.

2. (19-22) The need of wisdom.

Wisdom strengthens the wise
More than ten rulers of the city.
For *there is* not a just man on earth who does good
And does not sin.
Also do not take to heart everything people say,
Lest you hear your servant cursing you.
For many times, also, your own heart has known
That even you have cursed others.

a. **Wisdom strengthens the wise**: A wise man – even with an *under the sun* premise – will see and appreciate the value of **wisdom**, that it gives more strength **than ten rulers of the city**.

b. **There is not a just man on earth who does good and does not sin**: A wise man understands the sinfulness of man – and his own sinfulness.

c. **Do not take to heart everything people say...even you have cursed others**: Wisely, the Preacher knew that we tend to take the words of others about us too seriously. People often say unguarded things that are not deeply felt; *we* say such things about others and would not want them to **take to heart** what we said.

i. In his book *Lectures to My Students*, Charles Spurgeon gave a chapter to this verse, which he titled "The Blind Eye and the Deaf Ear." In that chapter he gave wise advice to pastors and Christian workers that they should sometimes (if not often) simply overlook unkind and thoughtless things others say and do. We would not want to be judged by our worst moments; we should not judge others by theirs.

ii. "The fact that we often speak ill of others should make us less open to take offence at what is said of ourselves, and prepared to expect unfavorable comments." (Deane)

3. (23-25) Frustration in seeking wisdom.

All this I have proved by wisdom.
I said, "I will be wise";
But it *was* far from me.
As for that which is far off and exceedingly deep,

Who can find it out?
I applied my heart to know,
To search and seek out wisdom and the reason *of things,*
To know the wickedness of folly,
Even of foolishness *and* madness.

a. **All this I have proved by wisdom. I said, "I will be wise"; but it was far from me**: As the Preacher gives wise advice for living, he understood that his desire to be wise was not always fulfilled with true wisdom.

i. "The honest admission of failure to find wisdom – of watching it in fact recede with every step one takes, discovering that none of our soundings ever gets to the bottom of things – this is, if not the beginning of wisdom, a good path to that beginning." (Kidner)

b. **I applied my heart to know, to search and seek out wisdom and the reason of things**: Given his *under the sun* premise, his meaningless life could not be made meaningful by the attainment of wisdom.

4. (26-29) Searching for wisdom, the Preacher sees man's sinfulness.

And I find more bitter than death
The woman whose heart *is* snares and nets,
Whose hands *are* fetters.
He who pleases God shall escape from her,
But the sinner shall be trapped by her.
"Here is what I have found," says the Preacher,
"*Adding* one thing to the other to find out the reason,
Which my soul still seeks but I cannot find:
One man among a thousand I have found,
But a woman among all these I have not found.
Truly, this only I have found:
That God made man upright,
But they have sought out many schemes."

a. **I find more bitter than death the woman whose heart is snares and nets, whose hands are fetters**: In his unsatisfying search for wisdom, Solomon understood that a woman could be a danger and a trap. It was important to not let that happen; **he who pleases God shall escape from her**.

i. **But the sinner shall be trapped by her**: "'In her,' in the snare which is herself." (Deane) "The wanton woman, that shame of her sex. A bitch, Moses calls her (Deuteronomy 23:18)." (Trapp)

ii. Knowing Solomon wrote this, it makes us wish we knew more about *when* Solomon wrote this; at what point in his life. We know from 1 Kings 11:4: *For it was so, when Solomon was old, that his wives turned his heart after other gods; and his heart was not loyal to the* LORD *his God.* Surely, Solomon himself was caught in these **snares** and **nets** and **fetters**.

iii. Those who think that Ecclesiastes is the statement of Solomon's repentance and evidence that he turned his heart back to *the* LORD *his God*, this section is Solomon's way of saying, "I understood my error and turned from it." Those who are unsure of Solomon's repentance will place the writing of Ecclesiastes earlier in his life.

iv. All in all it is a fascinating question, and one (in the mind of this writer) that has no definitive answer: Was Solomon one who pleased God in escaping from this trap, or was he the sinner **trapped by her**?

b. **I cannot find: One man among a thousand I have found. But a woman among all these I have not found**: Solomon could find a rare man in **a thousand** with wisdom; but not even one **woman**. This speaks more about Solomon's choice of female companionship than it does about the relative wisdom of men and women.

i. "His fruitless search for a woman he could trust may tell us as much about him and his approach, as about any of his acquaintances." (Kidner)

ii. "Such as he knew her to be in Oriental courts and homes, denied her proper position, degraded, uneducated, all natural affections crushed or underdeveloped, the plaything of her lord, to be flung aside at any moment. It is not surprising that Koheleth's impression of the female sex should be unfavorable." (Deane)

iii. "He found that a harem did not provide the appropriate companion for man. How much better he would have been with one good wife, such as he speaks of in Ecclesiastes 9:9 and Proverbs 31!" (Wright)

c. **This only I have found: That God made man upright, but they have sought out many schemes**: Solomon understood that God made man without sin, but man has – since the time of Adam – **sought out many schemes** of sin and rebellion against God.

i. We take Solomon's statement "**God made man upright**" not to refer to each individual, but to man as he was originally made, to Adam and Eve in the Garden of Eden. "He was created neither sinful, nor neutral, but *upright*, a word used of the state of the heart which is disposed to faithfulness or obedience." (Eaton)

ii. "Since futility was not the first word about our world, it no longer has to be the last." (Kidner)

Ecclesiastes 8 - Wisdom and Mystery

A. More good advice for life "under the sun"

1. (1-4) Wisdom in obeying and honoring the king.

Who *is* like a wise *man?*
And who knows the interpretation of a thing?
A man's wisdom makes his face shine,
And the sternness of his face is changed.

I *say,* "Keep the king's commandment for the sake of your oath to God. Do not be hasty to go from his presence. Do not take your stand for an evil thing, for he does whatever pleases him."

Where the word of a king *is, there is* power;
And who may say to him, "What are you doing?"

> a. **Who is like a wise man**: Solomon searched for a wise man, who knew **the interpretation of a thing**. Solomon knew that wisdom makes a man happier, even in an *under the sun* premise (**makes his face shine…the sternness of his face is changed**).

> > i. "The shining *face* generally speaks of favour (*cf.* Numbers 6:25). Here it speaks of the wise man who is visibly gracious in his demeanour, and (as the next phrase says) whose gentleness is obvious in his facial expression." (Eaton)

> b. **Keep the king's commandment for the sake of your oath to God**: The Preacher understood what the Apostle Paul would later write in Romans 13 – that we should obey government authority as part of our obedience to God.

> > i. We do this primarily not to honor the **king** or government authority (though this is part of our obligation). Primarily, we honor government authority **for the sake of** our **oath to God**. In a New Covenant context, we do it as part of our obedience to God.

ii. "You have sworn obedience to him; keep your oath, for the engagement was made in the *presence of God*. It appears that the Jewish princes and chiefs took an oath of fidelity to their kings. This appears to have been done to *David*, 2 Samuel 5:1-3; to *Joash*, 2 Kings 11:17; and to *Solomon*, 1 Chronicles 29:24." (Clarke)

iii. We can agree with Solomon's advice here, from both an Old Testament and New Testament perspective. Yet one must say that it sounds self-serving coming from Solomon, who was a king himself.

iv. We also recognize that we are always to obey God rather than man if the two contradict (Acts 4:19). "Many passages in the Old Testament witness to the limits which loyalty to God must set on courtly tact and submissiveness." (Kidner)

c. **Where the word of a king is, there is power; and who may say to him, "What are you doing"**: This is a reason why it is wise to obey a king. Their power – though sometimes held unrighteously – makes it unwise to fail to **keep the king's commandment** or show him respect.

i. This also makes us reflect on our obedience to God as the Great King. "If he be a King, then it is a solemn hazard to your soul if you come short of the least of his commandments. Remember that one treason makes a traitor; one leak sinks a ship; one fly spoils the whole box of ointment. He that bought us with his blood deserves to be obeyed in all things with all our heart, and mind, and soul, and strength." (Spurgeon)

2. (5-9) Reasons for wise living.

He who keeps his command will experience nothing harmful;
And a wise man's heart discerns both time and judgment,
Because for every matter there is a time and judgment,
Though the misery of man increases greatly.
For he does not know what will happen;
So who can tell him when it will occur?
No one has power over the spirit to retain the spirit,
And no one has power in the day of death.
There is no release from that war,
And wickedness will not deliver those who are given to it.

All this I have seen, and applied my heart to every work that is done under the sun: *There is* a time in which one man rules over another to his own hurt.

a. **He who keeps his command will experience nothing harmful**: Good will come to those who obey and honor the king.

b. **Because for every matter there is a time and judgment**: Wisdom knows what Solomon first poetically explained in Ecclesiastes 3:1-8 – that there is a time and purpose for everything under heaven.

c. **Though the misery of man increases greatly. For he does not know what will happen**: The Preacher understood that **for every matter there is a time and judgment**; but he also knew that we don't know what those times are. A wise man's heart may discern **both time and judgment**, but certainly not perfectly; and not all are wise.

> i. "The highest wisdom is submission to things as they are… Yet in doing all this there will abide in the heart the recognition of abounding injustice." (Morgan)

d. **No one has power over the spirit to retain the spirit, and no one has power in the day of death**: If the lack of wisdom discouraged Solomon in Ecclesiastes 8:6-7, he found the powerlessness of man in the face of death to be yet more despairing. *Under the sun*, he saw that **death** allows no winners, and **there is no release from that war**.

e. **All this I have seen…there is a time in which one man rules over another to his own hurt**: The Preacher knew that part of man's misery on this earth was to be ruled by others oppressively.

> i. "This may be spoken of rulers generally, who, instead of *feeding, fleece the flock*; tyrants and oppressors, who come to an untimely end by their mismanagement of the offices of the state. All these things relate to *Asiatic* despots, and have ever been more applicable to *them* than to any other sovereigns in the world. They were despotic; they still are so." (Clarke)

B. Even wisdom doesn't answer the big questions.

1. (10-13) Why are the deeds of the wicked soon forgotten?

Then I saw the wicked buried, who had come and gone from the place of holiness, and they were forgotten in the city where they had so done. This also *is* vanity. Because the sentence against an evil work is not executed speedily, therefore the heart of the sons of men is fully set in them to do evil. Though a sinner does evil a hundred *times,* and his *days* are prolonged, yet I surely know that it will be well with those who fear God, who fear before Him. But it will not be well with the wicked; nor will he prolong *his* days, *which are* as a shadow, because he does not fear before God.

a. **I saw the wicked buried…they were forgotten in the city where they had so done**: Solomon saw that the **wicked** die, and their evil is soon forgotten instead of being memorialized in infamy. With his *under the sun* premise, Solomon despaired that *the wicked dead are not punished after death*.

i. "I have seen wicked men buried and as their friends returned from the cemetery, having forgotten all the dead man's evil deeds, these men were praised in the very city where they had committed their crimes!" (Living Bible)

b. **Because the sentence against an evil work is not executed speedily, therefore the heart of the sons of men us fully set in them to do evil**: If wicked men are often not punished after death, they also are often not punished in this life. All this added to the sense of life's meaninglessness for Solomon.

i. This also speaks of the hardened response many make to the mercy and forbearance of God toward them. "Man's godless ingratitude is as deep a mystery as is God's loving patience. It is strange that, with such constant failure of His love to win, God should still persevere in it." (Maclaren)

c. **I surely know that it will be well with those who fear God, who fear before Him. But it will not be well with the wicked**: In context, we can suppose that the Preacher said this as a hope or a wish, rather than with real confidence. He *wishes* this were true but cannot have confidence that it is while clinging to his *under the sun* premise.

2. (14) Why do the bad have it good and the good have it bad?

There is a vanity which occurs on earth, that there are just *men* to whom it happens according to the work of the wicked; again, there are wicked *men* to whom it happens according to the work of the righteous. I said that this also *is* vanity.

a. **There are just men to whom it happens according to the wicked**: Solomon, speaking from his eternity-excluding viewpoint, felt this made life meaningless (**vanity**). Why do good men and women suffer?

i. This was the great question of the Book of Job, and almost unanswerable apart from a life that appreciates eternity and our accountability in the world beyond.

b. **Again, there are wicked men to whom it happens according to the work of the righteous**: Perhaps even more of a problem to the Preacher was the question, "Why do **wicked men** seem to be blessed?" The strength of this question also made life seem meaningless (**vanity**).

i. One might say that this question is even more troublesome, because in a very real sense, there are no **just men**, and all can be seen as

wicked in some way. Why goodness is shown to the undeserving is a question that looks to the remarkable mercy of God.

3. (15-17) Live for the moment – and know there is more than what you can see.

So I commended enjoyment, because a man has nothing better under the sun than to eat, drink, and be merry; for this will remain with him in his labor *all* **the days of his life which God gives him under the sun.**

When I applied my heart to know wisdom and to see the business that is done on earth, even though one sees no sleep day or night, then I saw all the work of God, that a man cannot find out the work that is done under the sun. For though a man labors to discover *it,* **yet he will not find** *it;* **moreover, though a wise** *man* **attempts to know** *it,* **he will not be able to find** *it.*

a. **So I commended enjoyment**: With the meaninglessness of life so plain to the Preacher, all he could counsel was to make the best of a bad situation and enjoy life the best way possible.

b. **Then I saw all the work of God, that a man cannot find out the work that is done under the sun**: Here Solomon begins to undermine his once-so-certain premise of life lived without an eternal perspective. He recognizes that man **cannot find out the work** of God in fullness; so what we see does not define what there actually is.

i. **The business that is done on earth, even though one sees no sleep day or night**: "The very busyness of life worries us into asking where it is taking us, and what it means, if it does mean anything. We hardly need Qoheleth to point out that this is the very question that defeats us." (Kidner)

ii. **He will not be able to find it**: "His conclusion is that we must be content not to know everything. Neither hard work (*toil*), persistent endeavour (*seeking*), skill or experience (*wisdom*) will unravel the mystery. Wise men may make excessive claims; they too will be baffled." (Eaton)

Ecclesiastes 9 - The Best Way to Live Under the Sun

A. In light of death, live life and make the best of a bad thing.

1. (1-6) The despair of death: the same thing happens to everyone.

For I considered all this in my heart, so that I could declare it all: that the righteous and the wise and their works *are* in the hand of God. People know neither love nor hatred *by* anything *they see* before them. All things *come* alike to all:

One event *happens* to the righteous and the wicked;
To the good, the clean, and the unclean;
To him who sacrifices and him who does not sacrifice.
As is the good, so *is* the sinner;
He who takes an oath as *he* who fears an oath.

This *is* an evil in all that is done under the sun: that one thing *happens* to all. Truly the hearts of the sons of men are full of evil; madness *is* in their hearts while they live, and after that *they go* to the dead. But for him who is joined to all the living there is hope, for a living dog is better than a dead lion.

For the living know that they will die;
But the dead know nothing,
And they have no more reward,
For the memory of them is forgotten.
Also their love, their hatred, and their envy have now perished;
Nevermore will they have a share
In anything done under the sun.

    a. **The righteous and the wise and their works are in the hand of God....**
    All things come alike to all: With his *under the sun* premise – excluding any sense of eternity or accountability in a life to come – man can **know**

neither love nor hatred by anything they see before them. Creation can tell us God is; it doesn't tell us very well that God loves us.

i. "We have only to use our eyes without prejudice, according to Psalm 19 and Romans 1:19 ff., to see that there is a powerful and glorious Creator. But it takes more than observation to discover how He is disposed towards us." (Kidner)

ii. Seeing beyond this *under the sun* perspective, we can say that we should not measure God's love by what happens in life. We measure God's love by what Jesus did at the cross.

ii. The Preacher has once again allowed his thoughts of God's sovereign power (**in the hand of God**) to develop into fatalism (**all things come alike to all**). The thought process may go like this: "I know God rules over all things." Then, "It seems that the same thing happens to all; all die without real meaning revealed for their life." Finally, "The all-powerful God means it to be this way."

b. **One event happens to the righteous and the wicked...as is the good, so is the sinner**: This develops Solomon's idea that all share the same destiny in this meaningless life of ours. This is certainly how things *appeared* to Solomon with his *under the sun* premise.

c. **This is an evil in all that is done under the sun**: Speaking from his premise, the Preacher *says* that all have the same fate, but *he does not like it*. It's wrong that **one event happens to the righteous and the wicked**.

i. "To all appearances, God is just not interested. The things that are supposed to matter most to Him turn out to make no difference – or none that anyone can see – to the way we are disposed of in the end. Moral or immoral, religious or profane, we are all mown down alike." (Kidner)

d. **For him who is joined to all the living there is hope, for a living dog is better than a dead lion**: This makes perfect sense from an *under the sun* perspective. If all existence and consciousness end with death, then the *only* thing that matters is this present life (and therefore nothing really matters).

e. **The dead know nothing...Nevermore will they have a share in anything done under the sun**: With great poetic effect, Solomon puts forth the belief that all existence and consciousness end with this life.

2. (7-10) With such a view of life and death, joy is only found in the moment.

Go, eat your bread with joy,
And drink your wine with a merry heart;
For God has already accepted your works.

Let your garments always be white,
And let your head lack no oil.

Live joyfully with the wife whom you love all the days of your vain life which He has given you under the sun, all your days of vanity; for that *is* your portion in life, and in the labor which you perform under the sun. Whatever your hand finds to do, do *it* with your might; for *there is* no work or device or knowledge or wisdom in the grave where you are going.

a. **Go, eat your bread with joy**: From outside of his *under the sun* premise, we see a touch of humor in the Preacher's analysis. "Life is utterly meaningless, and our common death and destiny prove it to be so. So forget about all I have said and have a good time." It is small hope given to despairing men and women, but it is the best he can do.

b. **For God has already accepted your works**: Given the recent emphasis on the sovereign power of God (Ecclesiastes 7:13, 9:1), we sense both fatalism and wishing in this statement. Perhaps the sense is, "**God has already accepted your works** – *I hope*; because if He hasn't, there is nothing you can do about it."

c. **Live joyfully with the wife whom you love all the days of your vain life which He has given you under the sun, all your days of vanity**: Clearly, Solomon knew that enjoying the good things at hand in this life – **bread, wine, garments**, comforts (**let your head lack no oil**), and a **wife whom you love** – none of these took away the meaninglessness of life. "Make **your vain life** a little better," he counseled.

i. "*White garments* and anointing *oil* make life more comfortable in a hot climate." (Eaton)

ii. "The demands of marriage include the giving of affection (*whom you love*; *cf.* Ephesians 5:25), the active quest for enjoyment (*Enjoy life*, rsv), a life-long (*all…your…life*) encouragement amid the responsibilities and duties of life (*in all your toil at which you toil*)." (Eaton)

d. **Whatever your hand finds to do, do it with your might; for there is no work or device or knowledge or wisdom in the grave where you are going**: The Preacher continued to give advice meant to make the best of the bad situation of life **under the sun**.

i. In the 1960s there was a beer commercial where the announcer said something like this: "You only go around once in life, so you've got to grab for all the gusto you can." The ad writers for Schlitz beer could have properly given credit to Solomon for the idea.

ii. We can apply the attitude reflected in Ecclesiastes 9:10 to our present service for God, and **do it with your might**. "No man ever served God by doing things tomorrow." (Spurgeon)

iii. "Man was not created to be idle, he was not elected to be idle, he was not redeemed to be idle, he was not quickened to be idle, and he is not sanctified by God's grace to be idle." (Spurgeon)

3. (11-12) Time and chance make life under the sun hard to understand.

I returned and saw under the sun that—
The race *is* not to the swift,
Nor the battle to the strong,
Nor bread to the wise,
Nor riches to men of understanding,
Nor favor to men of skill;
But time and chance happen to them all.
For man also does not know his time:
Like fish taken in a cruel net,
Like birds caught in a snare,
So the sons of men *are* snared in an evil time,
When it falls suddenly upon them.

a. **I returned and saw under the sun that – the race is not to the swift, nor the battle to the strong**: Solomon wondered, "If this life is all there is, then why doesn't this life make more sense?" In a world that made more sense **under the sun**, then the **swift** would always win the **race** and the **strong** would always win the **battle**. Yet it doesn't always work that way.

b. **But time and chance happen to them all**: The Preacher again struggles against a sense of fatalism. In his somewhat contradictory way, the one who previously proclaimed God's management of all (Ecclesiastes 7:13 and 9:1) now wondered if it didn't all happen according to **time and chance**.

i. "*Time and chance* are paired, no doubt because they both have a way of taking matters suddenly out of our hands." (Kidner)

c. **The sons of men are snared in an evil time, when it falls suddenly upon them**: From his **under the sun** perspective, it seemed that man was more subject to the whims of **time and chance** than of a loving, all-powerful God.

B. Unappreciated wisdom.

1. (13-15) Wisdom unrecognized.

This wisdom I have also seen under the sun, and it *seemed* great to me: *There was* a little city with few men in it; and a great king came against

it, besieged it, and built great snares around it. Now there was found in it a poor wise man, and he by his wisdom delivered the city. Yet no one remembered that same poor man.

a. **A poor wise man, and he by his wisdom delivered the city**: Solomon tells a story about a **poor wise man** whose **wisdom** saved a city against the siege of a **great king**. This **seemed great** to Solomon; it was a wonderful and significant display of wisdom.

b. **Yet no one remembered that same poor man**: Under the premise that death ends existence and consciousness for all, Solomon protested that the only lasting meaning this man might have – to be **remembered** – was taken away. The almost unbelievable fleetingness of fame added to the sense of meaninglessness of life.

i. Men quickly forget, but God never does. He knows those who are His (2 Timothy 2:19). He has a book of remembrance before Him for those that fear the Lord (Malachi 3:16), and their names are written in heaven (Luke 10:20).

2. (16-18) Wisdom thwarted.

Then I said:
"Wisdom *is* better than strength.
Nevertheless the poor man's wisdom *is* despised,
And his words are not heard.
Words of the wise, *spoken* quietly, *should be* heard
Rather than the shout of a ruler of fools.
Wisdom *is* better than weapons of war;
But one sinner destroys much good."

a. **Wisdom is better than strength**: The Preacher knew that even though wisdom is not appreciated, and it is ultimately vain, it was still **better than strength**.

b. **Words of the wise, spoken quietly, should be heard rather than the shout of a ruler of fools**: *Because* wisdom is superior, it should be heard above the shouts of the foolish – even though wisdom will often be unappreciated.

i. "The Preacher continues to emphasize the ease with which wisdom is counteracted." (Eaton)

c. **Wisdom is better than weapons of war; but one sinner destroys much good**: Wisdom is **better** – better than strength (**weapons of war**), better than foolishness – but all the good that wisdom does can quickly be taken away by **one sinner** who **destroys much good**.

i. Solomon sensed that it was much easier to destroy than to build. Establishing things by wisdom is much more difficult than destroying them by the work of even **one sinner**.

ii. "Adam's sin infected the whole race of man; Achan's transgression caused Israel's defeat (Joshua 7:11, 12); Rehoboam's folly occasioned the great schism (1 Kings 12:16)." (Deane)

Ecclesiastes 10 - Folly and Wisdom

A. The disgrace of foolishness.

1. (1) Foolishness disgraces a wise man's honor.

Dead flies putrefy the perfumer's ointment,
And cause it to give off a foul odor;
So does **a little folly to one respected for wisdom** *and* **honor.**

> a. **Dead flies putrefy the perfumer's ointment**: Solomon here followed a familiar form in stating proverbs. An obvious statement is made: that **dead flies** spoil a fine **ointment** and cause it to smell.

> > i. "This is a metaphorical confirmation of the truth enunciated at the end of the last chapter, 'One sinner destroyeth much good.'" (Deane)

> b. **So does a little folly to one respected for wisdom and honor**: Even as small dead flies – quite little in proportion to the whole – spoil a fine **ointment**, so just a **little folly** spoils the reputation of someone regarded as wise and honorable.

> > i. "There are endless instances of prizes forfeited and good beginning marred in a single reckless moment – not only by the irresponsible, such as Esau, but by the sorely tried, such as Moses and Aaron." (Kidner)

> > ii. The Preacher is beginning to direct his arguments in the intended direction. To use the metaphor of a ship, he has sailed in many different directions to show us the meaninglessness of life. Now, still out of sight of land, he begins to tack his direction towards meaning and truth. Ecclesiastes 10:1 reminds us that *even small things have consequences.*

2. (2-3) Foolishness can't be hidden.

A wise man's heart *is* **at his right hand,**
But a fool's heart at his left.
Even when a fool walks along the way,

He lacks wisdom,
And he shows everyone *that* he *is* a fool.

> a. **A wise man's heart is at his right hand, but a fool's heart at his left**: Since the **right hand** was regarded as the side of strength, skill, and favor, the **wise man's heart** is known and a strength to him. This is not true of the **fool**, whose **heart** is **at his left**.

> > i. "'Right' and 'left' are natural symbols for the strong and good, on the one hand, and for the weak and bad, on the other hand… The Latin word *sinister* means 'left.'" (Wright)

> > ii. "To have one's *heart at his left side* is to have the 'springs of life' (Proverbs 4:23) located in the realm of practical and spiritual incompetence." (Eaton)

> b. **He shows everyone that he is a fool**: The foolish man (or woman) has a way of making their folly evident. As Jesus would later say, *wisdom is justified by all her children* (Luke 7:25). Wisdom and folly become obvious in life.

3. (4-7) Foolishness in high places.

If the spirit of the ruler rises against you,
Do not leave your post;
For conciliation pacifies great offenses.
There is an evil I have seen under the sun,
As an error proceeding from the ruler:
Folly is set in great dignity,
While the rich sit in a lowly place.
I have seen servants on horses,
While princes walk on the ground like servants.

> a. **If the spirit of the ruler rises against you**: The idea seems to be, "Even in a difficult situation, don't **leave your post**. Be faithful to your position and you will find that **conciliation pacifies great offenses**."

> b. **Folly is set in dignity … I have seen servants on horses**: The Preacher wanted to remind us that *not all is fair in this life*. Foolish men are promoted or accepted to positions of great leadership. Some lowly men are unwisely exalted (**servants on horses**) while some noblemen are humbled (**princes walk on the ground like servants**).

B. Evidence of folly and wisdom.

1. (8-10) Foolishness in action.

He who digs a pit will fall into it,
And whoever breaks through a wall will be bitten by a serpent.

He who quarries stones may be hurt by them,
And he who splits wood may be endangered by it.
If the ax is dull,
And one does not sharpen the edge,
Then he must use more strength;
But wisdom brings success.

a. **He who digs a pit will fall into it**: Solomon listed several examples of those who did wrong or foolish things and then suffered because of it.

i. "While spoiling his neighbour's property, he himself may come to greater mischief." (Clarke)

ii. Alexander Maclaren made a spiritual application of the idea, **whoever breaks through a wall will be bitten by a serpent**: "Whoso pulls down the wall of temperance, a serpent will bite him. Trembling hands, broken constitutions, ruined reputations, vanished ambitions, wasted lives, poverty, shame, and enfeebled will, death – these are the serpents that bite, in many cases, the transgressor."

b. **If the ax is dull, and one does not sharpen the edge, then he must use more strength; but wisdom brings success**: The fool will continue to use a **dull** ax, instead of being wise and sharpening the edge. The fool doesn't wisely consider the future, and how wise use of one's time in the present can make for a much better future.

i. F.B. Meyer made a helpful application to the Christian worker of this by analogy: "There are times with all who work for God, when they are blunt, through much usage …. At all such times let us turn to God and say, 'Put in more strength. Let thy power be magnified in my weakness. Give more grace, so that thy work shall not suffer' …. Surely more work is done by a blunt edge and divine power, than by a sharp edge and little power."

2. (11-14) The babbling talk of the foolish.

A serpent may bite when _it is_ not charmed;
The babbler is no different.
The words of a wise man's mouth _are_ gracious,
But the lips of a fool shall swallow him up;
The words of his mouth begin with foolishness,
And the end of his talk _is_ raving madness.
A fool also multiplies words.
No man knows what is to be;
Who can tell him what will be after him?

a. **A serpent may bite when it is not charmed; the babbler is no different**: As dangerous as a biting serpent is the one who talks – babbles – like a fool. Though the **words of a wise man's mouth are gracious**, the **lips of a fool shall swallow him up**.

b. **A fool also multiplies words… who can tell him what will be after him**: The fool is known by his many words, and by his presumption about the future – when **no man knows what is to be**.

　　i. "The word for 'fool' here is *sakal*, which implies a dense, confused thinker." (Deane)

　　ii. Previously the Preacher had confidently stated that there is nothing beyond this life, and that this life should be lived with an *under the sun* premise. He now casts more doubt upon that premise.

3. (15) The fool at work.

The labor of fools wearies them,
For they do not even know how to go to the city!

a. **The labor of fools wearies them**: The fool has no desire to work; or when they do they quickly become wearied. They can't see that it is *wise to work now in order to prepare for the future*.

b. **They do not even know how to go to the city**: The Preacher continued to subtly back away from his previous *under the sun* premise. The fool has no sense of direction or goal. They live their life as if it were meaningless, directionless.

　　i. "The phrase, 'how to go to the city,' seems to be a kind of proverbial comparison for anything that is very plain and conspicuous." (Maclaren)

　　ii. "In a fine note of sarcasm, this proverb says that a person may be so involved in arguing about the universe that he misses what the ordinary person is concerned about, namely, finding the way home." (Wright)

　　iii. "To be ever learning, never arriving, as 2 Timothy 3:7 portrays some people, is to be a trifler who contrives to get lost on even the straightest *way to the city*. That is folly without even the excuse of ignorance." (Kidner)

4. (16-20) How foolishness corrupts a nation.

Woe to you, O land, when your king *is* a child,
And your princes feast in the morning!
Blessed *are* you, O land, when your king *is* the son of nobles,
And your princes feast at the proper time—
For strength and not for drunkenness!

Because of laziness the building decays,
And through idleness of hands the house leaks.
A feast is made for laughter,
And wine makes merry;
But money answers everything.
Do not curse the king, even in your thought;
Do not curse the rich, even in your bedroom;
For a bird of the air may carry your voice,
And a bird in flight may tell the matter.

a. **Woe to you, O land, when your king is a child**: Solomon himself felt that he was but a child when he came to the throne of Israel; therefore, he wisely asked God for the wisdom to lead a great people (1 Kings 3:7-9).

i. "A nation's first need is a mature leader. RSV *is a child* refers to age but to general maturity." (Eaton)

b. **Woe to you, O land … Blessed are you, O land**: The Preacher understood that a land was **blessed** by good, faithful leaders, but cursed under wicked and incompetent leaders.

i. **Because of laziness the building decays**: "Lazy rulers bring down the great house of the nation, as a lazy householder lets the beams of his house collapse so that the roof sags and lets in the rain." (Wright)

ii. If Ecclesiastes 10:18 pictures the fall of a nation, the following lines give the *reason* for fall – leaders who are foolish, selfish, and concerned only for their own pleasure and good.

iii. "They do nothing in order; turn night into day, and day into night; sleep when they should wake, and wake when they should sleep; attending more to chamberings and banquetings, than to the concerns of the state." (Clarke)

c. **A feast is made for laughter, and wine makes merry; but money answers everything**: Solomon here spoke in the voice of a wicked, unwise king. Along this line, he counseled his readers to not **curse the king** lest they be found out.

i. "Kings have long ears, heavy hands; walls also and hedges have ears." (Trapp)

ii. " 'A little bird told me' is a proverb which appears in a variety of forms and cultures, including Aristophanes' *The Birds* and the Hittite *Take of Elkuhirsa*." (Eaton)

iii. The thought is suggestive. A king may hear of my wrongdoing and I may suffer because of it, even though I did not know he could learn of it. *The same is true of my wrongdoing before God.*

Ecclesiastes 11 - Towards True Wisdom

A. Looking beyond what can be seen.

1. (1-2) Working for a profit that can't be immediately seen.

Cast your bread upon the waters,
For you will find it after many days.
Give a serving to seven, and also to eight,
For you do not know what evil will be on the earth.

a. **Cast your bread upon the waters**: This probably refers to a shipping venture that required great patience for the return of the investment. The idea is that it was wise and good to work for a return that could not be immediately seen.

i. "The allusion is to the element of trust in much ancient business. Ships on commercial voyages might be long delayed before any profit resulted." (Eaton)

ii. Some commentators (Trapp, Clarke, and others) think this speaks of generosity. **Cast your bread upon the waters** is to them a way of saying, "Give your material things to the needy in a way that might seem wasteful – as wasteful as throwing **bread upon the waters**, and you will be rewarded." If this is the sense, the point is much the same: do something now for a reward that cannot be immediately seen.

b. **Give a serving to seven, and also to eight, for you do not know what evil will be on the earth**: The Preacher counseled generosity and did so in light that the future – though uncertain – must be prepared for. With these ideas he continues to direct us towards the place of true wisdom.

i. " 'Give a portion to seven' is advice to use all opportunity speculatively, because one does not know what calamities may be ahead, and because it is well to have provided beforehand for such contingencies." (Morgan)

2. (3-4) Cause, effect, and the limits of analysis.

If the clouds are full of rain,
They empty *themselves* upon the earth;
And if a tree falls to the south or the north,
In the place where the tree falls, there it shall lie.
He who observes the wind will not sow,
And he who regards the clouds will not reap.

a. **If the clouds are full of rain, they empty themselves upon the earth**: With these proverbs Solomon emphasized the idea of cause and effect. This principle alone directs us toward eternity, because the wickedness or goodness of man in this earthly life is often not answered in this life. The necessary effect from that cause must be realized in eternity.

i. Clouds are designed to be **full of rain**, and therefore to **empty themselves upon the earth**. For Spurgeon, this idea of design and what comes from it suggested the work of Jesus for us: "Now, dear heart, if thou believest Christ to be a cloud that is full of rain, for what reason is he full? Why, that he may empty himself upon the earth. There was no need that he should be a man full of sympathy except to sympathize with mourning men and women. There was no need that he should bleed except that he might bleed for you. There was no necessity that he should die except that the power of his death might deliver you from death."

ii. **In the place where the tree falls, there it shall lie**: "Jerome's strange interpretation of the fallen tree has persisted, and some Christians have quoted it out of context. The tree, he said, is the dead person, and his destiny is fixed at death. But while this is true enough, it cannot be proved from this verse." (Wright)

b. **He who observes the wind will not sow**: The farmer who is overly analytical about **the wind** or **the clouds** will never plant his fields, and thus he **will not reap**. The Preacher gently pushes us away from an overly analytical approach to life.

i. "If we are always waiting for favouring conditions, we shall resemble the farmer who is ever looking out for perfect weather, and lets the whole autumn pass without one handful of grain reaching the furrows." (Meyer)

ii. "If we keep on observing circumstances, instead of trusting God, we shall be guilty of *disobedience*. God bids me sow: I do not sow, because the wind would blow some of my seed away. God bids me reap: I do not reap, because there is a black cloud there, and before I can house the harvest, some of it may be spoiled. I may say what I like; but I am guilty of disobedience." (Spurgeon)

iii. Spurgeon went on in that sermon (*Sowing in the Wind, Reaping Under Clouds*) to describe other ways that this attitude sins against God and man. To observe circumstances instead of trusting God shows *unbelief, rebellion, foolish fear,* and *idleness.*

B. Moving towards real wisdom, through fits and starts.

1. (5) The limitations of knowledge.

As you do not know what *is* the way of the wind,
***Or* how the bones *grow* in the womb of her who is with child,**
So you do not know the works of God who makes everything.

a. **As you do not know what is the way of the wind**: Solomon again reminds us of the limitations of human knowledge. We don't know **the way of the wind** or how **the bones grow in the womb** of a mother.

i. "Thus at this point in his closing appeal the Preacher simply insists on a fact: certain aspects of God's working on earth defy explanation. The mystery which shrouds our very origin underlies the whole of reality." (Eaton)

ii. As Jesus would later say, *The wind blows where it wishes, and you hear the sound of it, but cannot tell where it comes from and where it goes. So is everyone who is born of the Spirit* (John 3:8).

b. **So you do not know the works of God who makes everything**: In the same way we don't know the hidden things, we also do not know **the works of God** in any comprehensive way. The Preacher brings us to a place of humility and submission to God and His works that again pushes us out of the previously entrenched *under the sun* premise.

2. (6) Sowing seed with more trust than certainty.

In the morning sow your seed,
And in the evening do not withhold your hand;
For you do not know which will prosper,
Either this or that,
Or whether both alike *will be* good.

a. **In the morning sow your seed, and in the evening do not withhold your hand**: Using agricultural images, the Preacher tells us to do work of all kinds – the work one would do **in the morning**, and the work one would do **in the evening**.

i. "Some commentators have taken *Sow your seed* to refer to the begetting of children following the Talmud and Midrash, but this is hardly suitable to the context." (Eaton)

b. **For you do not know which will prosper**: Solomon again pushes towards an appropriately humble loss of self-confidence. *We should* give ourselves to all kinds of work because we **do not know** the results. We know less of the future than we think we do; this shakes the previously assured *under the sun* premise.

3. (7-8) A final flirtation with the *under the sun* premise.

Truly the light is sweet,
And *it is* pleasant for the eyes to behold the sun;
But if a man lives many years
***And* rejoices in them all,**
Yet let him remember the days of darkness,
For they will be many.
All that is coming *is* vanity.

a. **Truly the light is sweet, and it is pleasant for the eyes to behold the sun**: After repeatedly arguing from the premise expressed by the phrase *under the sun*, the Preacher once more expressed the idea before coming to his conclusions in the last chapter of Ecclesiastes.

b. **Yet let him remember the days of darkness**: The sun gives light, but the *under the sun* premise seemed to bring the Preacher (and us) into **days of darkness**; and if lived under that premise, those dark days **will be many** and there will be much **vanity** to come.

Ecclesiastes 12 - The Conclusion of The Matter

A. Life in light of eternity.

1. (11:9-11:10) Even in youth, remember that judgment will one day come.

Rejoice, O young man, in your youth,
And let your heart cheer you in the days of your youth;
Walk in the ways of your heart,
And in the sight of your eyes;
But know that for all these
God will bring you into judgment.
Therefore remove sorrow from your heart,
And put away evil from your flesh,
For childhood and youth *are* vanity.

a. **Rejoice, O young man, in your youth**: Perhaps this argued that Solomon now looked back from old age to the days of his youth, before an *under the sun* premise took a toll upon his life and mind. He hoped for better for his young readers.

i. Morgan, on the last portion of the book, beginning at 11:9: "Its first word, like the first word in the Manifesto of the King in later days, indicates the true thought and desire of God for man: 'Rejoice.'"

ii. This also indicates that in his conclusion, Solomon saw clearly that there was a place in **youth** (though not only there) in the legitimate pleasures and satisfactions of life. If the meaning of life was not found in the pursuit of pleasure (as in Ecclesiastes 2:10-11), it is also not found in asceticism and self-denial for its own sake.

iii. If we accept the truth of the next few lines; that there is more to life than what we can see – that there is an eternity and an eternal God to reckon with – then the legitimate pleasures of life *can* be enjoyed in the best sense. One doesn't try to find meaning in those pleasures, but simply some good seasoning for a life that finds its meaning in eternity and the eternal God.

iv. "In this frame of mind we can now turn to the delights of life … not as if they were opiates to tranquillize us, but as invigorating gifts of God." (Kidner)

v. "Rab, a Jewish teacher of the third century A.D., commented, 'Man will have to give account for all that he saw and did not enjoy.'" (Wright)

b. **Walk in the ways of your heart, and in the sight of your eyes; but know that for all these God will bring you into judgment**: Here the Preacher comes to the answer of his premise and his book. One may live according to their **heart** and by what they see; but they should not think that their own **heart** or **eyes** will be their judge. *There is a* **God** *in heaven who will* **bring** *all your life and works* **into judgment**.

i. "The statement is brief, for he knew nothing more than the fact, and could add nothing to it." (Deane)

ii. Here is the antidote and antithesis of the *under the sun* premise. Life is lived not only for this life but also for eternity, knowing that good will be rewarded and evil will be condemned perfectly by the **God** who **will bring you into judgment**. Literally, Solomon spoke of *the* **judgment**, referring to our great accountability before God.

iii. "His judicial activity is not 'the type of the blindfold maiden holding a balance in her hand' nor 'the cold neutrality of an impartial judge', but is rather the consuming energy in which God must bring about 'right'." (Eaton) *This makes everything full of meaning.*

c. **Therefore remove sorrow from your heart**: Living in light of eternity and the eternal God gives us hope for this life, not only for the life to come. It will **remove sorrow from** the **heart**.

i. The Apostle Paul knew this eternal perspective banished **sorrow from** the **heart** and later wrote, *Therefore, my beloved brethren, be steadfast, immovable, always abounding in the work of the Lord, knowing that your labor is not in vain in the Lord.* (1 Corinthians 15:58)

ii. Without this premise of eternity and the eternal God, life is vain and meaningless. The Apostle Paul understood this: *If in this life only we have hope in Christ, we are of all men the most pitiable* (1 Corinthians 15:19).

d. **And put away evil from your flesh**: Living in light of eternity and the eternal God also is an incentive to live a holy, godly life in our days on earth. We know that our good will be rewarded and blessed; not only in this life, but also in the life to come.

e. **For childhood and youth are vanity**: In an *under the sun* premise, **childhood and youth** are all that matter. This isn't true when we live in light of eternity and the eternal God.

2. (12:1) The value of remembering God and eternity in youth.

Remember now your Creator in the days of your youth,
Before the difficult days come,
And the years draw near when you say,
"I have no pleasure in them":

a. **Remember now your Creator**: The idea of the **Creator** is important. This is the first mention of God as **Creator**. To this point the Preacher worked hard to ignore the eternal God one must stand before in the future; yet he also refused to think about the **Creator** God who existed *before* he did. This self-imposed ignorance relieved the sense of accountability before the **Creator**, which still must be accounted for in the life to come.

i. "*Creator* is a plural form in Hebrew, suggesting greatness of majesty." (Eaton)

b. **Remember now your Creator in the days of your youth**: Solomon knew that **youth** are often those most likely to discount the reality of eternity and the eternal God. This is natural, but regrettable, in youth – they are often the most difficult to convince that this life is merely a brief prelude to eternity.

i. Adam Clarke suggested several practical and important points to draw from this exhortation, among them:

• You are not your own; you have no right to yourself. God made you; He is **your Creator**.

• **Remember** Him; *consider* that He is your Creator.

• Remember Him in your **youth**; do not fail to give God the first and the best.

ii. "The Preacher here exhorts them to remember God betimes, to gather manna in the morning of their lives, to present the first-fruits to God." (Trapp)

iii. "As in youth all the powers are more active and vigorous, so they are capable of superior enjoyments. *Faith, hope*, and *love*, will be in their best *tenor*, their greatest *vigour*, and in their *least encumbered state*. And it will be *easier* for you to *believe, hope, pray, love, obey*, and *bear your cross*, than it can be in old age and decrepitude." (Clarke)

c. **Before the difficult days come, and the years draw near when you say, "I have no pleasure in them"**: The Preacher advised young people to remember God and eternity **before** they suffered greatly by subjecting themselves to an *under the sun* premise and all the meaninglessness associated with it.

3. (2-5) A poetic description of advancing age.

While the sun and the light,
The moon and the stars,
Are not darkened,
And the clouds do not return after the rain;
In the day when the keepers of the house tremble,
And the strong men bow down;
When the grinders cease because they are few,
And those that look through the windows grow dim;
When the doors are shut in the streets,
And the sound of grinding is low;
When one rises up at the sound of a bird,
And all the daughters of music are brought low.
Also they are afraid of height,
And of terrors in the way;
When the almond tree blossoms,
The grasshopper is a burden,
And desire fails.
For man goes to his eternal home,
And the mourners go about the streets.

a. **While the sun and the light, the moon and the stars, are not darkened**: Most agree that what follows here is a poetic description of the effects of advancing age.

- The arms and hands that keep the body now begin to tremble (**the keepers of the house tremble**).

- The legs and knees begin to sag (**the strong men bow down**).

- Teeth are lost and chewing is more difficult (**the grinders cease because they are few**).

- The eyes are dimmed (**the windows grow dim**).

- The ears become weaker and weaker (**the sound of grinding is low**).

- Sleep becomes more difficult and one is easy wakened (**one rises up at the sound of a bird**).

- Singing and music are less appreciated (**the daughters of music are brought low**).

- One becomes more fearful in life (**afraid of height, and of terrors**).

- The hair becomes white (**the almond tree blossoms**).
- The once active become weak (**the grasshopper is a burden**).
- The passions and desires of life weaken and wane (**desire fails**).

  i. **Desire fails**: "The word rendered 'desire' is found nowhere else in the Old Testament and its meaning is disputed." (Deane) Although, Kidner states: "This is the point of the Hebrew expression, 'the caper-berry fails'. This berry was highly regarded as a stimulus to appetite and as an aphrodisiac."

b. **For man goes to his eternal home, and the mourners go about the streets**: At the end of man's advancing age is **his eternal home** – *not* the unknown grave and darkness. The Preacher has now set man's advancing age in connection with eternity, not vanity.

  i. We do well to remember that the Old Testament generally does not state the life and condition of man after this life with great certainty. Yet through his diligent searching, the Preacher has come to the right conclusion – that after this life, **man goes to his eternal home** as **the mourners go about the streets**.

  ii. "So this wonderful book closes with the enunciation of a truth found nowhere else so clearly defined in the Old Testament, and thus opens the way to the clearer light shed upon the awful future by the revelation of the gospel." (Deane)

4. (6-7) A final plea: Remember God before you go to life beyond the sun.

Remember your Creator **before the silver cord is loosed,**
Or the golden bowl is broken,
Or the pitcher shattered at the fountain,
Or the wheel broken at the well.
Then the dust will return to the earth as it was,
And the spirit will return to God who gave it.

  a. **Remember your Creator before the silver cord is loosed**: Solomon again pleads with his reader to remember God *before* this life is over, and he repeated a variety of metaphors to describe the ending of this life.

  i. "The image points to the value of life (*silver… gold*), and the drama in the end of a life whose pieces cannot be put together again." (Eaton)

b. **Then the dust will return to the earth as it was, and the spirit will return to God who gave it**: This is *why* it is so important to **remember your Creator** in this life; because when this life is over, one will answer to the eternal God and to eternity.

B. Conclusion: Eternity and the eternal God make everything matter.

1. (8) A final analysis of life under the sun.

"Vanity of vanities," says the Preacher,
"All *is* vanity."

> a. **Vanity of vanities**: By way of contrast, the Preacher returned to his starting point (Ecclesiastes 1:2). Having examined the meaninglessness of life with an *under the sun* premise (excluding eternity and the eternal God), one *must* say that life is not only meaningless, but the ultimate in meaninglessness (**vanity of vanities**).

> b. **All is vanity**: With the *under the sun* premise, not only is life meaningless, but **all is vanity**. *Nothing* has meaning.

>> i. One man who reflected deeply on the meaning of life – and the price of a life lived without meaning – was a holocaust survivor named Viktor Frankl. His book *Man's Search for Meaning* relates some of his war experiences and understanding of life. He wrote:

>> ii. "This striving to find a meaning in one's life is the primary motivational force in man." "I think the meaning of our existence is not invented by ourselves, but rather detected." (Frankl)

>> iii. "I turn to the detrimental influence of that feeling of which so many patients complain today, namely, the feeling of the total and ultimately meaninglessness of their lives. They lack the awareness of a meaning worth living for. They are haunted by the experience of their inner emptiness, a void within themselves…. This existential vacuum manifests itself mainly in a state of boredom." (Frankl)

>> iv. Frankl warned of the danger of those who live without meaning: "No instinct tells him what he has to do, and no tradition tells him what he ought to do; sometimes he does not even know what he wishes to do. Instead, he either wishes to do what other people do (conformism) or he does what other people wish him to do (totalitarianism)."

>> v. Frankl was not a Christian and didn't believe there was any one meaning to life. He thought that each man had his own and it could even change from moment to moment. He thought that the meaning of life could be found in three ways. First, by doing a deed. Second, by experiencing a value. Third, by suffering.

2. (9-12) The Preacher prods us towards true wisdom.

And moreover, because the Preacher was wise, he still taught the people knowledge; yes, he pondered and sought out *and* set in order many proverbs. The Preacher sought to find acceptable words; and *what was*

written *was* upright—words of truth. The words of the wise are like goads, and the words of scholars are like well-driven nails, given by one Shepherd. And further, my son, be admonished by these. Of making many books *there is* no end, and much study *is* wearisome to the flesh.

a. **Because the Preacher was wise, he still taught the people**: The Preacher's search for knowledge didn't leave him less wise. He was still a teacher of **the people** and a writer of **proverbs**.

b. **The words of the wise are like goads, and the words of scholars are like well driven nails**: The Preacher kept his confidence in the power of words to teach, challenge, and change people. Special confidence was appropriate in those words **given by one Shepherd**, even if they came through a **wise** man or a **scholar**.

i. The Preacher understood how one should proclaim God's truth.

- He should teach **the people knowledge**.
- He should seek **to find acceptable words**.
- He should seek to bring forth that which is **upright – words of truth**.
- He should make his words as **goads** and **well-driven nails**, with point and direction.
- He should bring forth the words **given by one Shepherd**.
- He should realize that good **study is wearisome to the flesh** and be willing to pay that price.

ii. **Goads ... well-driven nails**: "Here then are two more qualities that mark the pointed sayings of the wise: they spur the will and stick in the memory." (Kidner)

iii. "He realized that *pleasing words* (lit. 'words of delight') have a penetrating effect that slapdash and ill-considered words lack. Second, his words are written *uprightly*. The two characteristics balance each other. His words are not so *pleasing* that they cease to be *upright*." (Eaton)

iv. "This eloquent man took pains that he might be heard with understanding, with obedience." (Trapp)

c. **Be admonished by these**: One should take special care to hear and **be admonished** by the words of God, **given by one Shepherd**.

d. **Of making many books there is no end, and much study is wearisome to the flesh**: The Preacher cautions us to not believe everything we read, for all does not come from the **one Shepherd**.

i. "We grow addicted to research itself, in love with our own hard questions. An answer would spoil everything." (Kidner)

ii. "Two thousand years have elapsed since this was written; and since that time some millions of treatises have been added, on all kinds of subjects, to those which have gone before. The press is still groaning under and teeming with books, books innumerable; and no one subject is yet *exhausted*, notwithstanding all that has been written on it." (Clarke)

3. (13-14) Conclusion: live as one preparing for judgment and eternity

Let us hear the conclusion of the whole matter:
Fear God and keep His commandments,
For this is man's all.
For God will bring every work into judgment,
Including every secret thing,
Whether good or evil.

a. **Let us hear the conclusion of the whole matter**: After writing much of the Book of Ecclesiastes from a common but false premise, one that excluded eternal accountability and the God of eternity, now the Preacher concludes, having led us to **the conclusion of the whole matter**.

b. **Fear God and keep His commandments, for this is man's all**: Solomon came to understand that it *was* worth it to obey God, and this obedience both pleased God and fulfilled man's destiny.

i. "*Fear God* is a call that puts us in our place, and all other fears, hopes, and admirations in their place." (Kidner)

ii. "From that to this should be every man's pilgrimage in this world. We begin at vanity, and never know perfectly that we are vain till we come to fear God and keep his commandments." (Trapp)

iii. "If it is the 'beginning of wisdom' it is also *the end*, the conclusion; no progress in the believer's life leaves it behind." (Eaton)

iv. "This is the only place in Ecclesiastes where the *commands* of God are mentioned." (Eaton)

v. The King James Version (and other translations as well) inserted an unhelpful word in Ecclesiastes 12:13, translating *For this is the whole duty of man*. The word *duty* does not appear in the Hebrew text, and it has much more the idea of **for this is man's all**.

vi. "The last phrase reads literally: 'For this is the whole of the man.' Elsewhere in Ecclesiastes, however, the 'whole of the man' is a Hebrew idiom for 'every man' (*cf* 3:13; 5:19). The sense, therefore, is 'This applies to everyone'." (Eaton)

c. **For God will bring every work into judgment, including every secret thing, whether good or evil**: This is impossible to say with an *under the sun* premise; yet it is the root reason why it is wise and good for man to **fear God and keep His commandments**.

i. There is, and will be, and eternal accounting for everything we do. This is the complete opposite of believing that all is vanity or meaningless; it means that *everything* has meaning and importance, both for the present and for eternity. "If God cares as much as this, nothing can be pointless." (Kidner)

ii. Through this book the Preacher carefully thought through (and lived through) a premise commonly held: of life lived without consideration of eternity and the eternal God. After all that, he comes to this conclusion – and challenges all those who continue holding to the premise he held through most all the book. "What would it be like, asks the Preacher, if things were utterly different from what you thought? What if this world is not the ultimate one? What if God exists and is a rewarder of those who seek him?" (Eaton)

iii. As Paul explained, this puts life into perspective: *For our light affliction, which is but for a moment, is working for us a far more exceeding and eternal weight of glory, while we do not look at the things which are seen, but at the things which are not seen. For the things which are seen are temporary, but the things which are not seen are eternal. For we know that if our earthly house, this tent, is destroyed, we have a building from God, a house not made with hands, eternal in the heavens. For in this we groan, earnestly desiring to be clothed with our habitation which is from heaven.* (2 Corinthians 4:17-5:2)

iv. "This is how the book will end. On this rock we can be destroyed; but it is rock, not quicksand. There is the chance to build." (Kidner)

v. In the 1930s an Australian alcoholic named Arthur Stace was converted and heard an inspiring sermon on the subject of *eternity*. The preacher said, "I wish I could shout ETERNITY through all the streets of Sydney!" Stace was so moved that as he left the church he felt an immediate urge to write the word *Eternity*; he had a piece of chalk in his pocket and bent down and wrote on the pavement. Stace was hardly literate and could barely write his own name legibly; but when he wrote *Eternity*, he did so in elegant copperplate style script, usually about 2 feet wide on the pavement. He spent the rest of his life – until 1967 – waking each day at about 5:30, praying for an hour or so, then going around Sydney where he felt God led him to write *Eternity* all over the city. Solomon would have approved of both Arthur Stace and his message: *Eternity*.

Song of Solomon 1 - "Rightly Do They Love You"

A. Introduction to the Maiden, the Beloved, and the daughters of Jerusalem.

1. (1) Title: The Song of All Songs.

The song of songs, which _is_ Solomon's.

> a. **The song of songs**: This great song, or collection of poetic songs, is unique in the Bible. If the Song of Solomon was not in our Bible and we were to discover it as an ancient document from the time of Solomon, it is unlikely that we would include it in the collection of Old Testament books.

>> i. "If a manuscript of this little book were found alone, detached from the biblical context and tradition, it undoubtedly would be viewed as secular. The book has no obvious religious content." (Kinlaw)

>> ii. It seems that Bible translators cannot even agree on a _name_ for the book. Some call it "Song of Solomon," some "Song of Songs," some even use the Latin word for _songs_, calling it "Canticles."

>> iii. No matter what one calls this book it has rightly been highly praised, even by those who have interpreted it in somewhat allegorical and speculative ways. "The entire history of the world from it beginning to this very day does not outshine that day on which this book was given to Israel. All the Scriptures, indeed, are holy...but the Song of Songs is the Holy of Holies." (Rabbi Aqiba, an early Jewish commentator on Song of Solomon, cited in Kinlaw)

>> iv. Charles Spurgeon preached 59 sermons on this book (in Victorian England) and Bernard of Clairvaux (1090-1153) preached 86 sermons on chapters one and two alone.

> b. **The song of songs**: Many different interpretive approaches have been used in understanding this great song.

>> i. Some avoid this book altogether. Origen (c.185-c.254), an important teacher in the early church, said of the Song of Solomon: "I advise

and counsel everyone who is not yet rid of vexations of the flesh and blood, and has not ceased to feel the passions of this bodily nature, to refrain from reading the book and the things that will be said about it." Origen apparently felt he was prepared to study Song of Solomon because he castrated himself when he was a young man.

ii. Others embrace this book with great devotion but see it primarily as an allegory describing the love relationship between God and His people, not between a husband and wife. "The early Jewish rabbis taught that the book pictures God's love for Israel. Early Christian writers took the same approach, but they replaced Israel with the Church. One writer in the third century wrote a ten-volume commentary on Song of Solomon, telling how the book describes God's love for Christians." (Estes) Trapp expresses this perspective: "The chief speakers are not Solomon and the Shulamite...but Christ and his Church."

iii. Others see this book primarily as a drama dealing with three characters; Solomon, a simple country shepherd, and the young maiden. The idea is that Solomon one day traveled through his kingdom and saw the young maiden and was captivated by her beauty. Though she was betrothed to the simple shepherd, Solomon brought her back to his palace and tried to win her affection with all lavish gifts and loving words. Though her resolve wavered, just before she gave in to Solomon's attention and affection, she fled his palace and went back to her simple shepherd, her true love.

iv. The best way to see this book is as a literal, powerful description of the romantic and sensual love between a man and a woman, observing both their courtship and their marriage. It does not give us a smooth chronological story, beginning with the introduction of the couple to one another and ending with their married life together. Instead, it is a collection of "snapshots" of their courting and married life, with the pictures not necessarily in order.

v. Yet, because God deliberately uses the marriage relationship as an illustration of the relationship that He has with His people, we find that this great **song of songs** *illustrates* the love, the intensity, and the beauty of relationship that should exist between God and the believer. This is clearly a *secondary* meaning, sublimated to the plain literal meaning, yet nevertheless valid and important.

vi. "There are those who treat this Book as a song of human love. There are those who consider its only value is that of its mystical suggestiveness. Personally, I believe that both values are here." (Morgan)

c. **The song of songs**: The fact that this "greatest of all songs" focuses on romance and marital love shows us what a high regard God has for the institution of marriage. We might expect that the **songs of songs** be a song that only praises God instead of one that celebrates love and sensuality within marriage.

i. This idea is decidedly contrary to the negative view towards marriage that came early in the history of the church. In 325 at the Council of Nicea, a proposal was made to prohibit all clergy from living as married; but the Council did not approve the proposal. In 386 Pope Siricius commanded that all priests live as celibates, and later this order was extended to include deacons in the church. In this period, many people who were ordained as priests were already married. Leo the Great (440-461), out of concern for these wives, did not allow priests to put their wives away but commanded that the priest and his wife live together as brother and sister – that is, without any sexual relationship. This command led to the rule that a married man could not be ordained as a priest unless he and his wife took a vow that they would live as celibate, and then led further to the refusal to ordain anyone who was or had been married.

ii. This idea that the *truly spiritual* cannot or should not be married and enjoy sexual love is not based in the Old Testament. The Old Testament has no word for a bachelor; in Old Testament thinking, there were to be none. Every patriarch was married, all priests were married, and as far as we know every prophet was married except for Jeremiah, who was uniquely commanded by God not to marry (Jeremiah 16:2). Since the office of high priest was hereditary, the high priest *had* to marry, showing that only a married man could experience this most intimate closeness and communion with God as the high priest did by entering the Most Holy Place on the Day of Atonement.

iii. As well, the idea that the *truly spiritual* cannot or should not be married and enjoy sexual love is not based in the New Testament. In the New Testament, Jesus reaffirmed the value of marriage in Matthew 19:3-9 when the religious leaders came to Him with a question about divorce. Hebrews 13:4 tells us that the marriage bed – understood as the place of sexual relations in marriage – is undefiled and should be honored by all. Paul told us that it was desirable for elders and church leaders to be married (1 Timothy 3:4 and Titus 1:6-7). Jesus began His ministry by blessing a wedding (John 3:29-30), and the final step in man's relationship and fellowship with God is pictured as a wedding feast (Revelation 19:6-10).

iv. The difference between the Old and New Testaments is that the New will allow that the unmarried state can also be good and even sometimes, in rare cases, preferable. We have the example of Jesus Himself (and later Paul, as in 1 Corinthians 7:7). Jesus also said that the state of a eunuch for the Kingdom of Heaven could be good (Matthew 19:11-12), and Paul recognized that singleness could be an advantage in a time of distress (1 Corinthians 7:26), but *never* commanded. The Old Testament virtually (not actually) forbids singleness; the New Testament allows it for those who are so gifted and called and encourages them to use their singleness for God's glory (1 Corinthians 7:32-35) – while all the while assuming the married state for the vast majority of Christians and Christian leaders.

v. "The Bible does not see marriage as an inferior state, a concession to human weakness. Nor does it see the normal physical love within that relationship as necessarily impure. Marriage was instituted before the Fall by God with the command that the first couple become one flesh. Therefore physical love within that conjugal union is good, is God's will, and should be a delight to both partners (Proverbs 5:15-19; 1 Corinthians 7:3)." (Kindlaw)

vi. Additionally, "The prospect of children is not necessary to justify sexual love in marriage. Significantly, the Song of Songs makes no reference to procreation." (Kinlaw)

vii. Nevertheless, over hundreds and hundreds of years in Christianity, the dominant view was that sexual passion and true spirituality were contradictory and opposed to each other. This idea that for the truly spiritual sexuality was repressed led to a greater emphasis on the idea that we are to be passionately devoted to Jesus Christ as a superior replacement of our sexual desires. "The result of this perspective was that the medieval church had a love affair with the Song of Songs. An eroticism precluded at the human level was permitted at the divine. No book of Scripture received such attention between Augustine and Luther. What Galatians was to the Reformers, the Song of Songs was to the church for a thousand years." (Kinlaw)

viii. We remind ourselves: "The book never claims to be an allegory. Other genuine allegories in the Bible (e.g., Ezekiel 17:23; Galatians 4:22-31) clearly symbolize truths outside the story. Song of Solomon presents itself, instead, as a literal account of the love of a man and a woman." (Estes) "Allegorical writing usually gives hints that it is allegory. The places are fabulous – Doubting Castle, The Slough of Despond, Puritania, Orgiastica; the names are obviously symbolic –

Mr Worldly Wiseman, Giant Despair, Mr Reason, the Clevers; and the story-line moves through obvious stages of climax and resolution. None of these is present in the Song of Songs." (Carr)

ix. Additionally, there is significant danger in emphasizing an allegorical approach for *interpretation*, more than just *application*. "Allegory, however, is too often uncertain, unreliable, and by no means safe for supporting faith. Too frequently it depends upon human guesswork and opinion; and if one leans on it, one will lean on a staff made of Egyptian reed [Ezekiel 29:6]." (Luther, cited in Kinlaw) Yet, even Luther had a hard time taking the Song of Solomon literally. "He saw in the bride a happy and peaceful Israel under Solomon's rule." (Kinlaw)

x. The purely allegorical approach to the Song of Solomon is wrong; yet it cannot be denied that since it presents the height and glory and passion of love in marriage, it powerfully *illustrates* the love-relationship that exists between God and His people, between Jesus Christ and His Church. "The songs should be treated first as simple and yet sublime songs of human affection. When they are thus understood, reverently the thought may be lifted into the higher value of setting forth the joys of communion between the spirit of man and the Spirit of God, and ultimately between the Church and Christ." (Morgan)

d. **Which is Solomon's**: We learn that Solomon, the son of David and one of the great kings of ancient Israel, composed this song. Solomon composed some 1,005 songs (1 Kings 4:32), and this was the greatest (**the song of songs**) among them.

i. Solomon is presumed to be the author because he is mentioned six times (Song of Solomon 1:5, 3:7, 3:9, 3:11, 8:11, and 8:12) and there are three references to an unnamed king (Song of Solomon 1:4, 1:12, and 7:5).

ii. The mention of Solomon brings up another problem with understanding the Song of Solomon; mainly, who are the characters speaking in this collection of poems, and how do we assign specific speaking lines to the specific characters? It must be admitted that the assignment of certain lines to certain individuals is somewhat subjective and will differ from translator to translator.

iii. As mentioned before, some people see this as a drama proving that true love wins out between the young maiden and simple country shepherd, even though Solomon tried to take the maiden for Himself. This would mean that there are four main speakers or characters in the song (including the "chorus" of the daughters of Jerusalem).

iv. It is the opinion of this commentator that there are actually only three main characters or speakers: the young maiden (*the Shulamite*), the young man (Solomon, *the Beloved*), and the chorus (*the Daughters of Jerusalem*). In addition to these main characters or speakers, there are also a few "minor" characters, including the brothers of the Shulamite and some relatives to the wedding party.

v. The young maiden is often called *the Shulamite*. "The girl is usually identified as a country girl from Shunem, a small agricultural village in Lower Galilee…. Some commentators suggest that she is one of Solomon's many wives, perhaps even the Egyptian princess described in 1 Kings 3:1; 7:8." (Carr)

vi. The young man is often called *the Beloved* and is generally identified with Solomon. It's curious that God used Solomon to write this, because in the big picture he miserably failed the tests of love and romance. Believing that the Song of Solomon really is by Solomon, we are left with difficult and perhaps unanswerable questions, such as: What is the occasion upon which it was written? Who is the woman so passionately loved by this man who ended with 700 wives and 300 concubines (1 Kings 11:3)? Why was this exceedingly wise man not wise enough to keep his affections for this special maiden alone?

vii. Perhaps the Song of Solomon does not reflect Solomon's actual experience – certainly not in an enduring sense – but his wise analysis and skillful presentation of the glory of romantic and sensual love; more in theory than in his enduring experience. Solomon was not the first nor the last wise man that lived as a fool when it came to romance and sexuality.

2. (2-4a) Opening words of the maiden.

Let him kiss me with the kisses of his mouth—
For your love *is* better than wine.
Because of the fragrance of your good ointments,
Your name *is* ointment poured forth;
Therefore the virgins love you.
Draw me away!

a. **Let him kiss me with the kisses of his mouth**: The dialogue between the maiden and the young man begins with this passionate desire of the maiden. She wants to receive and experience the love of her beloved.

i. At the very beginning, we catch some of the power of this Song of Solomon. One can learn many relationship principles from this book, but it is not presented to us primarily as a handbook on relationships.

"It does not state principles in logical arguments. Instead, it assembles a number of songs, or poems.... It causes us to *feel* as if we are with Solomon and Shulamith, not merely watching them. As we read, we share their feelings." (Estes)

ii. Uncomfortable with such strong passion expressed in sacred Scripture, many commentators minimize the strong desire of this book. As the old Puritan commentator John Trapp said of this verse: "She must have Christ, or else she dies; she must have the 'kisses of Christ's mouth,' even those sweet pledges of love in his Word, or she cannot be contented, but will complain."

iii. "No one can kiss two persons at the same time, so this is a matter of personal significance. Moreover, this kind of kiss is not on the cheek like that of Judas Iscariot, nor is it a kiss upon the feet like that of Mary, but it is 'the kisses of his mouth,' which would express a most personal and intimate love." (Nee)

b. **Let him kiss me with the kisses of his mouth**: Right away we are struck with two complementary truths regarding this loving couple. First, the maiden is not weak and passive; second, the young man is nevertheless a leader and respected as such.

i. This is undeniably a strong woman – who happens to do most of the talking through the Song of Solomon. "Nearly twice as many verses are from her lips than from his.... There is nothing here of the aggressive male and the reluctant or victimized female. They are one in their desires because their desires are God-given." (Carr)

ii. Yet we see that the young man occupies a place of leadership; she does not initiate a kiss but asks that he might kiss her. She asks that he draw her.

b. **For your love is better than wine**: To the maiden, the **love** of her beloved is more refreshing and intoxicating **than wine**. She is deeply, passionately infatuated with her man.

i. "The theme of sexual enjoyment and consummation runs through the book, and the theme of commitment is central to that whole relationship. This is no passing encounter: this is total dedication and permanent obligation." (Carr)

ii. Charles Spurgeon, the great preacher of Victorian England, followed the custom of his age and understood the Song of Solomon primarily as a poetic description of the love relationship between Jesus Christ and His people. In his sermon titled *Better than Wine*, he drew forth two main points:

Christ's love is better than wine because of what it is not:

- It is totally safe and may be taken without question – you can't take too much.
- It doesn't cost anything.
- Taking more of it does not diminish the taste of it.
- It is totally without impurities and will never turn sour.
- It produces no ill effects.

Christ's love is better than wine because of what it is:

- Like wine, the love of Christ has healing properties.
- Like wine, the love of Christ is associated with giving strength.
- Like wine, the love of Christ is a symbol of joy.
- Like wine, the love of Christ exhilarates the soul.

c. **Your name is ointment poured forth**: This expresses the respect and esteem the maiden had for the *character* and *reputation* of her beloved. The **name** represented much more than just the title by which her beloved was addressed; it represented his character and reputation. His **name** was like **ointment poured forth** and flowed from **the fragrance of** his **good ointments**.

i. "When she said that his name was 'perfume poured forth,' she meant that his character was as fragrant and refreshing as cologne poured out of a bottle. This is the reason the girls around the palace loved him – not just because he was handsome...but because his inner person was so attractive." (Glickman)

ii. This couple is obviously physically attracted to each other; yet their relationship goes far deeper. "From the start they focused on the other's character and kindness toward each other. They learned to value and care for each other as persons." (Estes)

iii. This shows us that a wise woman chooses a man whom *others* see to be a man of character. There is something not-quite-right if *she* thinks she can see what an amazing guy he is, but no one else can see it.

iv. The seriousness of her estimation of him – going far deeper than just a physical or sexual attraction – shows us the character of their passionate love. Reading this collection of love poems, one might easily think that this is primarily a book about *falling in love*. Instead, it is much more accurately seen as a book about *building love*.

d. **Therefore the virgins love you**: The maiden understood that *others* could see the good character qualities in her beloved, without necessarily being romantically attracted to him. This made her love him all the more.

e. **Draw me away**: This was the logical desire of a woman so taken with loving desire towards her beloved. She wanted to be *with him*, and to be *one with him*.

3. (4b) An interjection from the "Daughters of Jerusalem."

We will run after you.

a. **We will run after you**: The "**we**" of this verse is somewhat hard to identify, and as mentioned previously, the assignment of particular lines to particular characters through this collection of poems is somewhat subjective and may differ from translation to translation. The New King James translation assigns this line to the "Daughters of Jerusalem."

b. **We will run after you**: The idea is that the Daughters of Jerusalem – this on-looking chorus, who observe and celebrate the love between the maiden and the young man – they want to see what will happen as this wonderful love builds and takes its course. *It is a good thing*, and from their respectful distance they want to be part of it.

4. (4c) The Shulamite enters the king's chamber.

The king has brought me into his chambers.

a. **The king**: This is another line that seems to reinforce the point that this is Solomon, inviting the young maiden into the private rooms of his palace.

b. **The king has brought me into his chambers**: However, because it does not seem that their love is yet consummated, this reference to **his chambers** may well be poetic and symbolic, in the sense of "He has welcomed me into the affections and secrets of his heart."

5. (4d) The Daughters of Jerusalem remark on the couple and their love.

We will be glad and rejoice in you.
We will remember your love more than wine.

a. **We will be glad and rejoice in you**: The Daughters of Jerusalem rightly saw this passionate love as something to celebrate. It was *good* – not simply fun or exciting and should be recognized as such.

b. **We will remember your love more than wine**: Another phrase remarking on the beauty and goodness of their love.

6. (4e-6) The Shulamite considers her own shortcomings in appearance.

Rightly do they love you.
I *am* dark, but lovely,
O daughters of Jerusalem,
Like the tents of Kedar,
Like the curtains of Solomon.
Do not look upon me, because I *am* dark,
Because the sun has tanned me.
My mother's sons were angry with me;
They made me the keeper of the vineyards,
***But* my own vineyard I have not kept.**

a. **Rightly do they love you. I am dark**: Hearing the words of the Daughters of Jerusalem in the previous lines, the maiden considers that their high estimation of her beloved is appropriate (**Rightly do they love you**). Yet of herself, she feels that her deeply tanned appearance (**I am dark...like the tents of Kedar**) makes her less worthy of their praise and (presumably) of her beloved's attention.

i. The maiden was happy that the character of her beloved was good and could be seen as so. "Because his character was so attractive, the girl who will someday be his bride can confidently say that the women of the court *rightly* appreciate him. After they praise him, she must agree, 'Rightly do they love you.'" (Glickman)

ii. This well-deserved (**rightly**) respect others had for the young man showed that the maiden made a wise choice. "She should not be so infatuated that she imagines a scoundrel or knave to be her knight in shining armor. She should be able to say, 'rightly do I love you.' He should be the kind of person one ought to respect." (Glickman)

iii. Marriage-eligible women today should have the same perspective, considering that the Apostle Paul summarized the responsibility of a wife towards her husband in Ephesians 5:33 with one word: *respect*. Though it is common – in the words of a modern film – for women to select a man for who he *almost is*, or to choose him for the man *she can make him to be*, this is unwise. An unmarried woman should ask herself the serious question: "Can I genuinely respect this man as he is right now? Do I respect him enough to submit to him the way the Bible says a wife should submit?" The maiden of the Song of Solomon had already asked and answered this question.

b. **I am dark, but lovely**: The self-doubt the maiden had regarding her own appearance should not be overstated. She did feel, in some ways, unattractive and unworthy (**Do not look upon me, because I am dark**). Yet at the same time she could say she is **lovely**.

i. **Look not upon me**: "This is an attitude very common to early Christian life. We do not want our natural life to be exposed at all. Thus, before being sufficiently dealt with by the Holy Spirit, immature believers will tend to hide from others. They do not wish to be known as they really are." (Nee)

c. **Because the sun has tanned me**: Perhaps it is best to say that she saw herself as fundamentally **lovely**, yet marred by her prolonged exposure in the sun, transforming her more fair skin into darker, deeply tanned skin.

i. **Like the tents of Kedar**: "Kedar was a territory southeast of Damascus where the Bedouin roamed. Their tents were made of the skins of black goats." (Kinlaw)

ii. In that day (as in most of history), fair skin was considered more attractive than tanned skin, because it showed that one was of a financial or social status high enough to where they did not have to perform outdoor work; they lived a higher life than that of simple farmers.

iii. The manner in which primarily allegorical interpreters deal with the line, **because the sun has tanned me**, demonstrates the weakness of the primarily allegorical approach. Trapp discusses how some think that **the sun** represents the Sun of Righteousness, Jesus Christ, and how in His brilliance the church sees its own nothingness. Or, he says that **the sun** might represent original sin. But he thinks the best understanding is to see **the sun** as "the heat of persecution, and the parching of oppression."

d. **My mother's sons were angry with me; they made me the keeper of the vineyards**: Worse still for the maiden, her unattractive appearance was unjustly forced upon her by her stepbrothers. Somewhat as a "Cinderella" figure, she was forced to work by cruel relatives.

i. The maiden seems to make – or at least almost makes – the mistake of thinking that her hardships have disfigured her and make her less qualified to be truly loved. Instead, "She has a natural attractiveness to her and a certain humility which often only suffering can bring. No doubt genuineness and humility were refreshing changes to the king." (Glickman)

e. **But my own vineyard I have not kept**: She worked hard in this unjust labor, while neglecting her own appearance. In this she well represents the thinking of many women who consider themselves not attractive enough to be truly and passionately loved. She should not believe the lie that her hardships have made her less attractive to a good man.

i. There is an old story about a thief who broke into a department store and stole nothing; but he switched the price tags. The next day an expensive Swiss watch was marked as being worth $1.50; a fine leather handbag was marked for $1.75. A simple rubber ball for a child was marked for $150.00 and three pencils were marked for $175.00. If people bought or sold at those prices, you would think they were crazy. Yet *all the time* people value precious attributes and characteristics in other people very cheaply (especially when it comes to love and romance), and they assign high value to attributes and characteristics that are actually worth little.

B. Endearing words between young lovers.

1. (7) The Shulamite speaks to her beloved.

Tell me, O you whom I love,
Where you feed *your flock,*
Where you make *it* rest at noon.
For why should I be as one who veils herself
By the flocks of your companions?

a. **Tell me, O you whom I love, where you feed your flock**: Here the beloved is pictured as a shepherd, which was presumably a symbolic representation, perhaps touching on the idea common in the ancient world that the king was like a shepherd to his people. Yet the picture is clear: she wanted to know where her beloved was, because she simply wanted to be *with him.*

i. This picture of a shepherd is one reason why some think that the Song of Solomon is actually a drama with a distinction between Solomon the king and the beloved who is also a simple shepherd. On balance, it seems best to regard this simply as a poetic description of Solomon the king, who was also the beloved.

b. **For why should I be as one who veils herself**: Here the maiden proclaims her modesty, because in that culture a *veiled woman* was a woman of low sexual morals. She didn't want to make herself look like a loose girl following the **flocks** looking for any lover; therefore, she wanted to know where her beloved was. She didn't want *a* man; she wanted *her* man, her *special* man, her beloved.

i. Genesis 38:13-15 tells us that when Tamar, the widow of the sons of Judah wanted to entrap her father-in-law Judah by posing as a prostitute, she *covered herself with a veil and wrapped herself, and sat in an open place.* This was making herself available as a prostitute.

ii. "In their culture this term, 'a veiled woman,' referred to a loose girl, likely a prostitute. If she were going to see the king, she wanted it to be at the proper time and place – say, for example, when he was free in the middle of the day. She didn't want to go wandering around looking for him, appearing to be an aggressive and available prostitute to everyone else." (Glickman)

iii. In this the maiden shows that she is both *humble* (in that she doesn't want to make an ostentatious search for her beloved) and she has *integrity*, not wanting to even *appear* like one of these "loose girls." She understood that when it comes to sexual attraction and reputation, what others think *does* matter.

2. (8-10) The beloved praises his lover.

If you do not know, O fairest among women,
Follow in the footsteps of the flock,
And feed your little goats
Beside the shepherds' tents.
I have compared you, my love,
To my filly among Pharaoh's chariots.
Your cheeks are lovely with ornaments,
Your neck with chains *of gold.*

a. **If you do not know, O fairest among women, follow in the footsteps of the flock**: Poetically, the beloved tells the maiden where she can find him – just follow the flocks. He welcomes her presence and companionship and is happy to have her with him.

b. **To my filly among Pharaoh's chariots**: Historical studies set this phrase in an interesting light. Normally, we would think of a beautiful **filly**, magnificently drawing **Pharaoh's chariots**. Yet there are ancient sources that indicate that by strict rule, **Pharaoh's chariots** were pulled by *stallions*, not fillies, mares, or geldings. This then would have the sense that the maiden was as alluring and exciting as a filly among stallions.

i. Estes describes the more conventional view: "Solomon's mare was his pride and joy. It was the most beautiful and graceful horse in the kingdom. It had been specially selected to draw the king's chariot... only one horse was good enough for Solomon. The meaning of the comparison is obvious; other women may be fine, but Shulamith was the only one Solomon prized." (Estes)

ii. Yet it seems that by the middle of the second millennium before Christ – well before the time of Solomon – the custom was established that only two stallions pulled the chariot of Pharaoh (according to

Carr and others). Here, the man describes his wife as a **filly among Pharaoh's chariots**, which probably means that she had the same sexual attraction that a mare loose among stallions would have.

c. **Your cheeks are lovely with ornaments, your neck with chains of gold**: The beloved praised the beauty of the maiden in general (as in Song of Solomon 1:15). Here, more specifically, he praised the way that she made herself beautiful, with **ornaments** on her **cheeks** and **chains of gold** on her **neck**.

3. (11) The daughters of Jerusalem offer gifts to the Shulamite.

We will make you ornaments of gold
With studs of silver.

a. **We will make you ornaments of gold**: The on-looking daughters of Jerusalem wanted to bless the maiden also. When they saw how the king cared for her, they wanted to be kind and good to her also.

i. This is one reason why it is important to a woman that her man treat her well and treat her well in public. She instinctively understands that others will treat her better if they see that her man values her and treats her well.

b. **Ornaments of gold with studs of silver**: This shows how greatly they responded to the example set by the beloved. His treatment of the maiden made them want to be somewhat extravagant in honoring the maiden.

i. "In all probability, she was not in actual possession of any of these items. Rather, they are similes that express her sweet feelings toward her lover." (Carr)

4. (12-14) The Shulamite describes how precious her beloved is to her.

While the king *is* **at his table,**
My spikenard sends forth its fragrance.
A bundle of myrrh *is* **my beloved to me,**
That lies all night between my breasts.
My beloved *is* **to me a cluster of henna** *blooms*
In the vineyards of En Gedi.

a. **While the king is at his table, my spikenard sends forth its fragrance**: The maiden was aware of her attractive powers, and how her attractiveness could draw her beloved (**the king**) to herself. This is clearly a woman who is aware of her sexual attractiveness but uses it in a godly and responsible manner; not for casual flirtation or questionable liaisons.

b. **A bundle of myrrh is my beloved to me**: The maiden understood her ability to attract her beloved; and she also understood his ability to attract her. This dynamic of mutual romantic and sexual attraction is wonderful in the context of a concern for character and corresponding commitment; it is a dangerous dynamic outside this context.

c. **That lies all night between my breasts**: The idea is that the presence and scent of her beloved stayed with her, even when the maiden was alone. The thought of her lover is like a fragrance that stays with her and sustains her, even when he is not there.

> i. "Shulamith was explaining that even while she slept alone at night, Solomon's love continued to enrich and nourish her life." (Estes)

> ii. This speaks to the sense of *security* that his love gives to her. Since she is secure in his love, he doesn't need to be immediately there for her to be blessed and benefited by it.

d. **Between my breasts**: This reference to the female breast – made by the maiden herself – makes some readers and commentators of the Song of Solomon uncomfortable. There is a reflexive instinct to believe that God *must* have had something else in mind; something more *spiritual*.

> i. "Jewish scholars have seen in the bride's breasts Moses and Aaron; the two Messiahs, Messiah Son of David and Messiah son of Ephriam; Moses and Phinehas; and Joshua and Eleazar. Christian interpreters have been equally ingenious. They have seen the bride's breasts as the church from which we feed; the two testaments, Old and New; the twin precepts of love of God and neighbor; and the Blood and the Water. Gregory of Nyssa found in them the outer and the inner man, united in one sentient being." (Kinlaw)

d. **In the vineyards of En Gedi**: The place known as **En Gedi** is a famous oasis in the Judean wilderness, lush with water and life in an otherwise barren place. **A cluster of henna blooms in the vineyards of En Gedi** would be alive, beautiful, healthy, and full of good scents.

> i. "The king was En-Gedi to this girl, an oasis of life in a desert of monotony, and like a weary traveler she found refreshment with him." (Glickman)

5. (15) The Beloved praises the beauty of the Shulamite.

Behold, you *are* fair, my love!
Behold, you *are* fair!
You *have* dove's eyes.

a. **Behold, you are fair, my love**: With both the intensity of the words and their repetition, we see that the beloved lavished praise upon the maiden for her beauty. It was important for him to say and for her to hear; *she was beautiful to him.*

b. **You have dove's eyes**: He especially noted the beauty in her *eyes*. It is true that some women have beautiful eyes by birth; yet there is something wonderful about the beauty of spirit that is seen in the eyes. A woman deeply in love with God has a particular beauty in her **eyes**.

i. "The large and beautiful dove of Syria is supposed to be here referred to, the eyes of which are remarkably fine." (Clarke)

6. (16-17) The Shulamite responds with kind words.

Behold, you *are* handsome, my beloved!
Yes, pleasant!
Also our bed *is* green.
The beams of our houses *are* cedar,
***And* our rafters of fir.**

a. **Behold, you are handsome, my beloved**: The maiden loved and respected the character of her **beloved** (Song of Solomon 1:3); yet she was also attracted to his appearance. This was no doubt because the **beloved** was and made himself **handsome**; but also, because she saw him through a woman's eyes of love, which undeniably make a man better looking.

i. She is clearly responding to *his* previous expressions of love. "He calls her 'beautiful' (1:15); she responds with the masculine form of the same Hebrew word (1:16)." (Kinlaw)

b. **The beams of our houses are cedar, and our rafters of fir**: The image is as if they are on a walk in the country, and the use the plants and scenes around them as pictures of their love and relationship.

Song of Solomon 2 - "My Beloved Is Mine and I Am His"

A. The maiden and her beloved continue to praise each other.

1. (1) The maiden describes herself to her beloved.

I *am* the rose of Sharon,
And the lily of the valleys.

> a. **I am the rose of Sharon**: Her view of herself has remarkably changed. In the first visits at the palace, she was self-conscious and unsure of her appearance and worth. Now she says, "**I am the rose of Sharon, and the lily of the valleys.**"

> > i. This is a line that commonly is attributed to the beloved, and then allegorically applied to Jesus Christ. Therefore, "Rose of Sharon" or "Lily of the Valley" is in many writings, songs, and minds a poetic title for Jesus Christ, reflecting His great beauty and glory. Unfortunately, this is a decidedly wrong understanding; these words are rightly attributed to the maiden in the New King James translation.

> > ii. Spurgeon was one who took this mistaken approach to the text and considered the idea of Jesus proclaiming His own beauty and greatness to us: "If a man praises his wares, it is that he may sell them. If a doctor advertises his cures, it is that other sick folk may be induced to try his medicine; and when our Lord Jesus Christ praises himself, it is a kind of holy advertisement by which he would tempt us to 'come, buy wine and milk without money and without price.' If he praises himself, it is that we may fall in love with him; and we need not be afraid to come and lay our poor hearts at his feet, and ask him to accept us." We might say that this is a wonderful point made from a misapplied text.

> b. **The rose of Sharon and the lily of the valleys**: She describes herself not as two flowers; yet they are two fairly commonplace wildflowers. She

regarded herself as a flower (definitely having beauty), but as rather plain flowers (not remarkable compared to others).

i. According to Trapp, the Septuagint translates **rose of Sharon** as *flower of the field*. We do know that **the rose of Sharon** describes not a proper rose, but a flower found in *the Sharon*, the low coastal plain stretching south from Mount Carmel in the northern part of Israel. The word translated **rose** here actually means "to form bulbs." Some think it refers to the bulb-like fruit produced by a rose bush, the rose hips. Yet according to Carr, "The general consensus is that the plant described here is one of the bulb family. Crocus, narcissus, iris, daffodil are the usual candidates."

ii. "*Sharon* was a very fruitful place, where David's cattle were fed, 1 Chronicles 27:29. It is mentioned as a place of excellence, Isaiah 35:2, and as a place of flocks, Isaiah 65:10." (Clarke)

iii. "The *lily of the valleys* is not our common white, bell-shaped plant of that name.... Some commentators, on the basis of Song 5:13, argue for a red or reddish-purple colour for the flower, but no identification is certain." (Carr)

iv. "Thus the Bride's description of herself was really self-depreciatory, rather than otherwise. It was as if she saw that there was nothing in her beauty extraordinary or out of the common." (Morgan)

2. (2) The beloved responds to the maiden.

Like a lily among the thorns,
So is my love among the daughters.

a. **Like a lily**: The beloved heard the maiden's almost confident self-description and responded with affirmation. Perhaps she said it with a touch of doubt, and he erased any doubt with his response.

i. Whatever the maiden might feel, *he* had no doubt about her beauty. "To the man, the wonder of his beloved is ever that she is full of beauty." (Morgan)

b. **Like a lily among the thorns, so is my love among the daughters**: The beloved added that the maiden was not only beautiful, but that she was also among those who didn't appreciate (or match) her beauty. The beloved gave his maiden a precious gift: the gift of feeling *preferred*. In his estimation, she was the flower and the other girls were just thorns.

i. "She is a *lily* indeed, but her beauty far surpasses the thorny weeds all around her." (Carr)

ii. "The bridegroom had just before called her *fair*; she with a becoming modesty, represents her beauty as nothing extraordinary, and compares herself to a *common flower of the field*. This, in the warmth of his affection, he denies, insisting that she as much surpasses all other maidens as the flower of the *lily* does the *bramble*." (Clarke)

3. (3) The maiden enjoys the loving presence of her beloved.

Like an apple tree among the trees of the woods,
So *is* my beloved among the sons.
I sat down in his shade with great delight,
And his fruit *was* sweet to my taste.

a. **Like an apple tree among the trees of the woods**: The language of trees and plants continues, now with the maiden describing her beloved as being like a large, healthy, life-giving **apple tree**.

i. "A humble wildflower herself, she recognizes her Bridegroom as a noble tree, alike ornamental and fruitful." (Taylor) Yet it is unlikely that Solomon had what we know as an apple tree in mind. "By the apple tree would probably be intended by the oriental writer either the citron, or the pomegranate, or the orange. I suppose he did not refer to the apple tree of our gardens, for it would scarcely be known to him." (Spurgeon)

ii. We sense the couple is busy complimenting each other. "I'm a simple wildflower." "No, you are a wildflower among the thorns." "You are like a beautiful apple tree" and so on.

b. **I sat down in his shade with great delight**: The maiden found a great sense of security and peace under the protective covering of her beloved. She felt sheltered and shaded; that she was no longer at the mercy of others, but now under his care.

i. Her feeling of security is directly connected to his openly proclaimed preference of her in the previous verse. She is not at the mercy of a man who might choose another woman at the slightest whim; she can feel secure in the love of a man who genuinely prefers her.

ii. "Whereas before she came to him she worked long hours in the sun (1:6), now she rests under the protective shade that he brings. And although formerly she was so exhausted by her work she could not properly care for herself, now she finds time for refreshment with him." (Glickman)

iii. **Sweet to my taste**: "*Taste* is more correctly *palate*, often including the lips, teeth, and the whole mouth. The Hebrew word for *discipline* or *training* (*hanak*) is derived from the same root. The first step in teaching a child is the anointing of his lips with honey so that learning is identified with sweetness." (Carr)

iv. Spurgeon gave an allegorical application to the idea of the maiden (representing God's people) resting under the shade of her beloved (representing Jesus): "Straightway she sat down under its shadow, with great delight, and its fruit was sweet unto her taste. She looked up at it; that was the first thing she did, and she perceived that it met her double want. The sun was hot, there was the shadow: she was faint, there was the fruit. Now, see how Jesus meets all the wants of all who come to him."

B. The maiden muses over her love relationship with her beloved.

In this section (Song of Solomon 2:4-17) the maiden – either in a dream or daydream – thinks about her beloved and the love they have shared and will share. The dialogue seems to completely belong to her in this section.

1. (4-7) The maiden thinks about the provision and intimacy she has found.

He brought me to the banqueting house,
And his banner over me *was* love.
Sustain me with cakes of raisins,
Refresh me with apples,
For I *am* lovesick.
His left hand *is* under my head,
And his right hand embraces me.
I charge you, O daughters of Jerusalem,
By the gazelles or by the does of the field,
Do not stir up nor awaken love
Until it pleases.

a. **He has brought me to the banqueting house**: The maiden dreamily thinks of her beloved bringing her to a special place, the **banqueting house** – which is more literally "house of wine," either in the sense of storage or production. It seems to be a secluded, outdoorsy place where the maiden and her beloved could be together and eventually be intimate.

i. "Idiomatically, the 'house of wine' could be the place where wine is grown (*i.e.* a vineyard), manufactured, stored, or consumed. The frequent use of the outdoor motifs in the Song, particularly of the garden as a place for the lovers' rendezvous, suggests that the vineyard itself is what is intended here." (Carr)

ii. "Literally, *the house of wine*. The ancients preserved their wine, not in barrels or dark cellars under ground, as we do, but in large *pitchers*, ranged against the wall in some upper apartment in the house, the place where they kept their most precious effects." (Clarke)

b. **His banner over me was love**: Taken more literally, this is a strange statement. Taken more poetically, the maiden rejoices that her beloved and publicly and openly proclaimed his love for her, as if he had set up a **banner** or flag to say it.

 i. "She is proclaiming that the love which the king has for her is evident to everyone. He does not say one thing to her in private and contradict that in public.... He is not ashamed of his love for her, so he is glad for all to see it." (Glickman)

 ii. "'His banner over me was love' suggests that the hoisting of this banner by her focuses the whole attention on love. It is a love relationship." (Nee)

 iii. "He is not ashamed to acknowledge her publicly.... The house of wine is now as appropriate as the King's chambers were. Fearlessly and without shame she can sit as His side, His acknowledged spouse, the bride of His choice." (Taylor)

c. **Sustain me with cakes of raisins, refresh me with apples**: She thought of enjoying food with her beloved in their outdoor rendezvous. Some commentators associate these foods with pagan fertility rites or aphrodisiac qualities, but this seems unwarranted and unnecessary.

d. **I am lovesick**: The maiden described a feeling familiar to many who have known the thrill of romantic love. She feels physically weak and perhaps even somewhat disoriented because of the strength of attraction and infatuation she has towards her beloved.

 i. According to Dr. Jeffrey Schloss, there is a brain hormone that mediates the feeling of being in love or being infatuated. One of these neurotransmitters is known as *phenethylamine*, and it floods our brain when we fall in love (it is also in fairly high quantities in chocolate). This chemical gives us feelings of exhilaration and thrill and well-being, and in high amounts can lead to a loss of appetite. This chemical works somewhat in a cycle, at least in a relationship. At the beginning of the relationship it spikes up; after four or five years it begins to decline. Across cultures there is spike in the rate of divorce at about 4.5 years of marriage.

 ii. This leads some scientists to say that we are made for monogamy, but only in the sense of one partner at a time, and then changing partners every five years or so. Yet Dr. Schloss says that we know this is not true. In the brain there are completely different pathways, with completely different chemical mediators. These begin to form at about the four-year point in a relationship, and they contribute to different feelings. Instead of feelings of thrill and "I can't eat," they are feelings of deep contentment and gratitude. One of the chemicals that mediates these feeling is *oxytocin*, which is the same chemical related to the bonding of a mother together with her infant.

iii. Some suggest that relationships have two major phases: *attraction* and *attachment*. The attraction phase is powerful, and the kind of condition that makes one say, "**I am lovesick**." Yet the key to a long-term fulfilling relationship is staying with it past the *attraction* phase into the *attachment* phase. There are some counselors who devote almost their entire counseling practice trying to help what they call "love junkies"; people who are so addicted to the *phenethylamine* phase that they bounce from relationship rush to relationship rush without ever really coming into a greater, longer lasting relationship fulfillment.

iv. One could say that we are engineered for the longer lasting *attachment* phase, and the *attraction* phase is meant to be a portal into the attachment phase, and not something unto itself. The good news is that as a relationship moves into the attachment phase, the attraction phase recycles, and long-married couples often experience the sense of falling in love all over again – several times through their marriage.

v. This is why it is sometimes – or often – unwise to rush ahead in a relationship when it is still in the "**I am lovesick**," attraction and *phenethylamine* phase. Adam Clarke observed of the **lovesick** person: "But while we admit such a person's sincerity, who can help questioning his judgment?"

vi. Watchman Nee applied this idea to the believer's relationship with God: "'Sick with love' is lovesickness, and is the equivalent of being exhausted with happiness. Such was the experience of the saints of all ages when they came into a full realization of the Lord's special presence."

e. **His left hand is under my head, and his right hand embraces me**: The maiden imagines herself and her beloved lying together and her beloved caressing her with **his right hand** (perhaps intimately).

i. **Embraces me**: "The word is not frequent in the Old Testament, and is used both of friendly greeting (Genesis 48:10) and of sexual union (Proverbs 5:20)." (Carr)

ii. "The position of the left hand *under* her head would suggest that the two are lying down and that with the right hand he is enfolding and caressing her." (Carr)

iii. "Enraptured in her love, Shulamith invited Solomon to enjoy her sexually. The language that she used here appears again in 4:6 and 8:14 in contexts that definitely refer to physical intimacy." (Estes)

iv. Since the maiden describes a dream or daydream, this describes her desire and not an action. "Here perhaps the RSV translation of Song of Solomon 2:6 is preferable: 'O that his left hand were under my head, and that his right hand embraced me!'" (Kinlaw)

f. **I charge you, O daughters of Jerusalem**: This exhortation to the **daughters of Jerusalem** is another reminder that this section (Song of Solomon 2:4-17) is to be understood as a dream or daydream of the maiden. We are not to imagine the couple together in the intimacy described in the previous lines (**his right hand embraces me**) with the **daughters of Jerusalem** standing around and taking note.

i. Yet here in her dream-like state, the maiden speaks to these imagined on looking **daughters of Jerusalem** and pleads with them (**I charge you**), vowing (or perhaps swearing) **by the gazelles or by the does of the field**. This poetic phrasing surely sounded more natural and meaningful to the first readers of the Song of Solomon than it does to us.

ii. "The adjuration which she used is a choice specimen of oriental poetry: she charges them, not as we should prosaically do, by everything that is sacred and true, but 'by the roes, and by the hinds of the field.'" (Spurgeon)

g. **Do not stir up nor awaken love until it pleases**: There are two meanings to the phrase in general. It could be, "Don't interrupt the sweet dream of love the maiden enjoys, drawing her back to the reality of daily life." Or it could be, "Don't start the process of loving exchange until the opportunity and appropriate occasion is present; don't start something unless we can complete it."

i. The idea is both plain and powerful. The maiden wants none of the onlookers to hinder or interrupt their love until it is fulfilled and consummated. We may say this is true both in the sense of their *relationship* and in the sense of their *passion*.

ii. In terms of relationship it means, "Let our love progress and grow until it is matured and fruitful, making a genuinely pleasing relationship – *don't let us go too fast*." "From her wish, an excellent principle can be drawn for courtship. A strong desire to express love physically should be present, but not until marriage should it be fulfilled. This restraint is healthy and beneficial to the couple." (Glickman) It is like letting a flower grow until it naturally blooms, instead of trying to force a flower to grow and blossom. This isn't *repression* – the rejection and denial of the feelings, often in shame; this is *suppression* – the conscious restraint of natural impulses and desires.

iii. In terms of passion it means, "Let our love making continue without interruption until we are both fulfilled. Don't let us start until we can go all the way."

2. (8-14) The maiden happily thinks over a visit from her beloved.

The voice of my beloved!
Behold, he comes
Leaping upon the mountains,
Skipping upon the hills.
My beloved is like a gazelle or a young stag.
Behold, he stands behind our wall;
He is looking through the windows,
Gazing through the lattice.
My beloved spoke, and said to me:
"Rise up, my love, my fair one,
And come away.
For lo, the winter is past,
The rain is over *and* gone.
The flowers appear on the earth;
The time of singing has come,
And the voice of the turtledove
Is heard in our land.
The fig tree puts forth her green figs,
And the vines *with* the tender grapes
Give a good smell.
Rise up, my love, my fair one,
And come away!
"O my dove, in the clefts of the rock,
In the secret *places* of the cliff,
Let me see your face,
Let me hear your voice;
For your voice *is* sweet,
And your face *is* lovely."

a. **The voice of my beloved**: Here the maiden moved to another scene in her dream or daydream. Before she imagined herself and her beloved at an outdoor rendezvous (Song of Solomon 2:4-7). Now she imagines a visit from her **beloved**, beginning with the idea that she is awakened or alerted by the sound of his **voice**.

b. **Behold, he comes leaping upon the mountains**: The maiden imagined her beloved bounding to come meet her, full of energy and excitement, as if he were **a gazelle or a young stag**.

c. **Behold he stands behind our wall; he is looking through the windows**: The maiden imagined her beloved peering through the windows to see if his maiden was home.

    i. "He was seen first *behind the wall*, and then in the *court*; and lastly came to the *window* of his bride's chamber." (Clarke)

d. **Rise up, my love, my fair one, and come away**: The maiden thought of her beloved inviting her out to enjoy the glory of spring, with the **rain... over and gone** and beautiful **flowers** and birds **singing**.

    i. "The season of spring reflects the experience of the young lovers. Everything is fresh; new life flows through the world; happiness and color triumph over winter's boring grays. Whenever any couple falls in love, it is spring for them." (Glickman)

    ii. **Voice of the turtledove**: "This species is primarily a migratory spring/summer resident of Palestine (*cf.* Jeremiah 8:7), whose distinctive cooing call is one of the signs of spring." (Carr)

    iii. **The fig tree puts forth her green figs**: "The fig tree in Judea bears *double* crops; the first of which is ripe in *spring*. But the tree, as I have elsewhere observed, bears figs all the year through, in the climes congenial to it. That is, the fig tree has always *ripe* or *unripe* fruit on it. I never saw a healthy tree naked." (Clark)

e. **Rise up, my love, my fair one, and come away**: The maiden dreamt of her beloved *insisting* that they enjoy the beauty of spring together. It was important for her to know that he *really* wanted to do this with her and did not do it reluctantly, as if he were simply willing to make himself miserable if it could please her. It was important for her to know that he really did simply want to *be with her*.

f. **O my dove...let me see your face**: The maiden imagined these sweet, impassioned words from her beloved (though it is also possible that she expressed them towards him). She dreamt that her special man would seek her out (**in the secret places of the cliff**) and would embrace her as someone **lovely** and beautiful.

i. **My dove**: "This word, here a pet name for the beloved…is the common Rock Dove, not the turtledove…the dove is a common symbol of love (the 'lovebird')." (Carr)

ii. **Let me see your face**, or more literally *appearance*. "He wants to feast his eyes on the loveliness of her whole person, and fill his ears with the pleasing sweetness of her *voice*." (Carr)

g. **For your voice is sweet**: The maiden considered how **sweet** and meaningful the sound of one's voice is between two lovers. She imagined her beloved longing to hear her voice and remembering how **sweet** the sound of it is.

i. The human voice has the amazing ability to communicate and connect. "The voice can invite or discourage intimacy, without ever having to be verbally explicit, or even conscious of what it is doing.… We use our voices to repel and attract, encourage or undermine. As animals with smell, so are humans with voices." (Anne Karpf, *The Human Voice*)

ii. Just hearing a human voice can give us information about a person's height, weight, shape, sex, age, occupation, sexual orientation, health, sobriety, tiredness, social class, race, education, financial status, and truthfulness. With all this power wrapped up in the voice, no wonder the maiden imagined her beloved saying to her, "**your voice is sweet**."

3. (15) The maiden's brothers warn of the "**little foxes**."

Catch us the foxes,
The little foxes that spoil the vines,
For our vines *have* tender grapes.

a. **Catch us the foxes**: It is somewhat difficult to understand who says these words, and to whom they are said. The translators of the New King James Version attribute them to the maiden's brothers; many others believe these words come from the maiden herself and are spoken to her beloved. The plural nature of the statement is clear; the idea is that **the foxes** will be caught together with another person (the brothers or the beloved), and not by one person working alone.

i. "This verse is a problem. The verb form is imperative, masculine plural, but there is no indication whether the speaker is male or female. All that is clear is that 'for us' is plural." (Carr)

b. **The little foxes that spoil the vines**: Clearly the maiden speaks poetically here, using the **little foxes** as emblems of that which would damage the love relationship she shares with her beloved. The idea is that their relationship is like a fruitful vineyard and the **little foxes** will damage the vineyard unless they are stopped and caught.

i. Glickman lists several "little foxes" that may trouble couples:

- Uncontrolled desire that drives a wedge of guilt and mistrust between the couple.

- Mistrust and jealousy that strains or breaks the bond of love.

- Selfishness and pride that refuses to acknowledge wrong and fault to one another.

- An unforgiving attitude that will not accept an apology.

ii. It is helpful to remember the wording of the verse: **catch us the foxes**. The job of catching foxes is *teamwork*. One partner in the relationship can't expect the other do it all.

iii. Hudson Taylor thought of the "**little foxes**" that may ruin our relationship with Jesus Christ. "The enemies may be small, but the mischief done great.... And how numerous the little foxes are! Little compromises with the world; disobedience to the still small voice in little things; little indulgences of the flesh to the neglect of duty; little strokes of policy; doing evil in little things that good may come; and the beauty, and the fruitfulness of the vine are sacrificed!"

c. **For our vines have tender grapes**: The maiden's idea is that their relationship is both especially precious (**tender grapes** are best) and vulnerable, needing protection (**tender grapes** need to be guarded).

i. "The appeal is made here to outsiders to prevent 'the foxes,' those forces that could destroy the purity of their love, from defiling their vineyards, which are blossoming.... So they plead for protection for the love that blossoms between them that nothing will spoil it." (Kinlaw)

ii. Thinking allegorically, Spurgeon considered aspects in the life of the believer that were like **tender grapes** that were in danger of being spoiled by the **little foxes**. He considered these to be **tender grapes** in the life of the believer:

- A secret mourning for sin.

- A humble faith in Jesus Christ.

- A genuine change of life.

- A life of secret devotion.

- An eager desire for more grace.

- A simple love to Jesus.

iii. "If you have any sign of spiritual life, if you have any tender grapes upon your branches, the devil and his foxes will be sure to be at you; therefore, endeavor to get as close as ever you can to two persons who are mentioned hard by my text, namely, the King and his spouse. First, keep close to Christ for this is your life; and next, keep close to his Church, for this is your comfort." (Spurgeon)

4. (16-17) The maiden thinks about her beloved.

Charles Spurgeon preached eight sermons on these two verses.

My beloved *is* mine, and I *am* his.
He feeds *his flock* among the lilies.
Until the day breaks
And the shadows flee away,
Turn, my beloved,
And be like a gazelle
Or a young stag
Upon the mountains of Bether.

a. **My beloved is mine, and I am his**: The maiden concludes this dreamy section confident in the bond that joins her and her beloved. He belongs to her, and she belongs to him. In this sense they are *one*, joined together with mutual bonds of affection, and not one partner clinging to another more reluctant partner.

i. It is also a statement of *exclusivity* and *preference*. They are *not* saying, "My beloved is mine, and I belong to him and a few other guys," nor "I am my beloved's and he is mine and he also belongs to 999 other women."

ii. Many people think the key to love is finding the perfect person; it is more a matter of finding the person who belongs to you, and you belong to them. "You don't look at the other person as a status symbol who will raise your prestige...you look at that one as your counterpart, the one who completes you, the one with whom you can joyfully affirm your belongingness." (Glickman)

iii. These lines have been repeatedly allegorically applied to the relationship between Jesus and His people. Charles Spurgeon preached eight sermons on Song of Solomon 2:16-17, and in one of them titled *The Interest of Christ and His People in Each Other*, he meditated on the meaning of each aspect.

iv. Ways that I belong to Jesus; ways that "**I am my beloved's**":

• I am His by the gift of His Father.

- I am His by purchase, paid for by His own life.

- I am His by conquest, He fought for me and won me.

- I am His by surrender, because I gave myself to Him.

- "Blessed be God, this is true *evermore* — 'I am his,' his to-day, in the house of worship, and his to-morrow in the house of business; his as a singer in the sanctuary, and his as a toiler in the workshop; his when I am preaching, and equally his when I am walking the streets; his while I live, his when I die; his when my soul ascends and my body lies mouldering in the grave; the whole personality of my manhood is altogether his for ever and for ever." (Spurgeon)

v. Ways that Jesus belongs to me; ways that "**He is mine**":

- He is mine by connection in the same body; He is the head and I am part of His body.

- He is mine by affectionate relationship; He has given me His love.

- He is mine by the connection of birth; I am born again of Him.

- He is mine by choice; He gave Himself for me.

- He is mine by indwelling; He has decided to live inside me.

- He is mine personally, He is mine eternally.

- "It certainly does seem a great thing to call him mine; to think that he should ever be mine, and that all he is, and all he has, and all he says, and all he does, and all he ever will be, is all mine. When a wife takes a husband to be hers, he becomes all hers, and she reckons that she has no divided possession in him; and it certainly is so with thee, dear heart, if Christ be thine." (Spurgeon)

vi. "Which is the greater miracle — that he should be mine, or that I should be his?" (Spurgeon)

b. **He feeds his flock among the lilies**: Lips are called **lilies** in Song of Solomon 5:13; the maiden probably dreamt of being smothered by kisses all through the night (**until the day breaks**).

i. "She is ready for him to 'graze' on her lips as sheep 'browse' on the lush grasses.... Perhaps this is to be related to the opening wish of our young lady (Song of Solomon 1:2)." (Kinlaw)

ii. Other commentators see something far less physically intimate: "She is drawing attention to his shepherd role wherein he would pasture his flock. And by this she emphasizes his shepherd-like qualities of strength and gentleness." (Glickman)

c. **Turn, my beloved, and be like a gazelle or a young stag**: The maiden dreamt of her beloved full of energy and virility, like a strong young **gazelle** or **stag**.

i. **The mountains of Bether** are very hard to identify. "The verbal root occurs twice in Genesis 15:10, where the meaning is obviously to divide an animal in a sacrificial ritual." (Carr) Therefore, the Jerusalem Bible translates this, *mountains of the covenant.*

ii. The phrase can also be translated, *mountains of division*. If this is the case, the thought may be that maiden longs for her beloved to **turn** and overcome the *mountains of division* as easily as if he were a **gazelle or a young stag**.

iii. "The spouse speaks of 'mountains' dividing her from her Beloved: she means that *the difficulties were great*. They were not little hills, but mountains, that closed up her way.... It is plain, from this sacred Canticle, that the spouse may love and be loved, may be confident in her Lord, and be fully assured of her possession of him, and yet, there may for the present be mountains between her and him." (Spurgeon)

Song of Solomon 3 - A Troubled Night, A Glorious Wedding Procession

A. The maiden searches for her beloved.

1. (1-3) The restless maiden searches for her beloved.

By night on my bed I sought the one I love;
I sought him, but I did not find him.
"I will rise now," *I said,*
"And go about the city;
In the streets and in the squares
I will seek the one I love."
I sought him, but I did not find him.
The watchmen who go about the city found me;
I said,
"Have you seen the one I love?"

a. **By night on my bed I sought the one I love**: The maiden woke in the middle of the night and instantly felt alone, longing for her beloved. She **sought him** but could not **find him** anywhere in the house.

i. This snapshot probably records another dream or daydream of the maiden, as in the previous chapter. With this section ending with her addressing her companions, we don't imagine that they haunted or stalked this loving couple with their actual presence at their intimacy.

ii. Since this is likely another dream or daydream of the maiden, it doesn't matter if she recorded it as a married woman or yet-to-be-married maiden. She had the longings of a married woman (that her beloved would share her home and her **bed**) but did not act upon those longings until married.

iii. These lines do record the sexual longing of the maiden, and this is indicated by the particular term used for **bed**: "This is the common word for bed, distinct from the word for 'couch' in 1:16. In Ezekiel 23:17 the connotation is 'love bed', and in Genesis 49:4 and Numbers 31:17ff is used with overt sexual meaning. This is its only use in the Song." (Carr)

iv. This connotation of the word for **bed** reminds us of Hebrews 13:4: *Marriage is honorable among all, and the bed undefiled; but fornicators and adulterers God will judge.* The Bible consistently condemns sex outside of the marriage commitment (*fornicators and adulterers God will judge*). But the Bible celebrates sexual love within the commitment of marriage, as indicated in The Song of Solomon.

b. **I sought him, but did not find him**: The maiden always longed for her beloved and wanted him close. Yet now, in the middle of the night, she felt the longing more intensely. She felt alone and longed for his presence, so she imagined herself seeking after him.

i. **Sought**: "Very common in the Old Testament, and is used both literally and figuratively. It is always a conscious act, frequently requiring a great deal of effort (*e.g.* 1 Samuel 10:14; Proverbs 2:4) but with no guarantee of success." (Carr)

ii. "This is very natural and very beautiful. Love creates a perpetual dread lest the loved one should be lost." (Morgan) "Love not only brings a greater experience of joy, but a deeper capacity for pain as well. So as the joy of the kings' presence became greater, so the sorrow from his absence became deeper." (Glickman)

iii. The maiden allowed herself to feel needy without feeling helpless. She felt that she needed her beloved and did not have an artificial sense of self-sufficiency. The maiden did not feel it was a bad thing for her to *need* her beloved.

iv. There is something good in the maiden's seeking of her beloved; yet it came after their relationship was well established. The relationship did not begin nor was it founded upon her pursuit of him.

v. "With what constancy she sought this communion. She began at dead of night, as indeed it is never too late to seek renewed fellowship. Yet she sought on. The streets were lonely, and it was a strange place for a woman to be at such a strange time, but she was too earnest in seeking to be abashed by such circumstances." (Spurgeon)

c. **I will rise...and go about the city...I will seek the one I love**: This emphasizes the urgency and depth of her seeking. She was safe (even under the supervision of the **watchmen**), but they could not help her find her beloved, even at her request.

i. "She did not sit down, and say to any one of them, "O watchman of the night, thy company cheers me! The streets are lonely and dangerous; but if thou art near, I feel perfectly safe, and I will be content to stay awhile with thee." Nay, but she leaves the watchmen, and still goes along the streets until she finds *him* whom her soul loveth." (Spurgeon)

ii. "It is probable that, lighting upon these watchmen, she promised herself much counsel and comfort from them, but was disappointed. It pleaseth God many times to cross our likeliest projects, that himself alone may be leaned upon." (Trapp)

2. (4) Finding her beloved.

Scarcely had I passed by them,
When I found the one I love.
I held him and would not let him go,
Until I had brought him to the house of my mother,
And into the chamber of her who conceived me.

a. **I found the one I love**: She dreamt that her diligent search was rewarded. Though the watchmen mentioned in the previous verse could not help her, she nevertheless **found the one** she loved.

i. It is repeated four times in these first four verses: **the one I love**. This is how she thought of her special man.

b. **I held him and would not let him go**: It is easy to picture the relieved maiden clinging to her beloved, feeling calmed and secure in his embrace.

i. **Would not let him go**: It seems to have been the same kind of embrace that Mary Magdalene had upon Jesus when she first saw her resurrected Lord (John 20:16-17).

ii. In either interpreting or applying Song of Solomon 3:1-4 to the relationship between Jesus and His people, many commentators have noted that this is an example of how the believer, under some sense of separation from Jesus, must seek after Him.

iii. "When, either in a dream, or in reality we lose our sense of His presence, let us search for Him; and then in the finding, with new devotion, let us hold Him, and refuse to let Him go." (Morgan)

c. **Until I had brought him to the house of my mother**: The maiden dreamed of bringing her beloved home with her, to always be together with him – and to enjoy the intimacy of **the chamber** of her mother's home.

i. "Still clinging to him, she leads him gently but forcefully to her mother's house and into the maternal bedroom." (Carr)

ii. The fact that it is in **the house of** her **mother** shows that she expected it to be when they were in fact married, and not as a pre-marital sexual rendezvous. "That there I might entertain and embrace him, and gain my mother's consent, and so proceed to the consummation of the marriage." (Poole)

iii. "She is not looking for an illicit consummation of their love. Consummation she wants, but even in her dream she wants the consummation to be right. Where in human literature does one find a text so erotic and yet so moral as this?" (Kinlaw)

iv. "This passage may also reflect ancient Israelite marital customs now unknown to us. Perhaps we should notice that Isaac brought Rebekah into the tent of his mother, even though Sarah was deceased, and there consummated their marriage (Genesis 24:67)." (Kinlaw)

v. Applying this symbolically, Charles Spurgeon noted the steps of the maiden's progress towards her beloved:

- She *loved him*.
- She *sought him*.
- She *found him not*.
- She *found him*.
- She *held him*.
- She *brought him*.

vi. Spurgeon also made great application of the fact that the maiden **held him and would not let him go**. "Mark, that according to the text, it is very apparent that Jesus will go away if he is not held. 'I held him and I would not let him go;' as if he would have gone if he had not been firmly retained. When he met with Jacob that night at the Jabbok, he said, 'Let me go.' He would not go without Jacob's letting him, but he would have gone if Jacob had loosed his hold. The patriarch replied, 'I will not let thee go, except thou bless me.' This is one of Christ's ways and manners; it is one of the peculiarities of his character. When he walked to Emmaus with the two disciples, 'he made as if he would have gone further:' they might have known it was none other than the Angel of the Covenant by that very habit. He would have gone further, but they constrained him, saying, 'Abide with us for the day is far spent.' If you are willing to lose Christ's company he is never intrusive, he will go away from you, and leave you till you know his value and begin to pine for him. 'I will go,' says he, 'and return to my place, till they acknowledge their offense, and seek my face: in their affliction they will seek me early.' He will go unless you hold him." (Spurgeon)

- Jesus *must* be held; He will go unless you hold Him.
- Jesus is *willing* to be held; He is not trying to escape us.
- Jesus *can* be held; He we can grasp Him by faith.
- Jesus *Himself* must be held; not merely a creed, tradition, or a ceremony.

3. (5) An exhortation to the maiden's companions.

I charge you, O daughters of Jerusalem,
By the gazelles or by the does of the field,
Do not stir up nor awaken love
Until it pleases.

a. **I charge you, O daughters of Jerusalem**: This exhortation to the **daughters of Jerusalem** is another reminder that this section is to be understood as a dream or daydream of the maiden. We are not to imagine the couple together in the intimacy described in the previous lines with the **daughters of Jerusalem** observing.

b. **By the gazelles or by the does of the field**: This poetic phrasing (first found in Song of Solomon 2:7) surely sounded more natural and meaningful to the first readers of the Song of Solomon than it does to us

c. **Do not stir up nor awaken love until it pleases**: As in its previous usage, this idea can be understood as a plea to leave her sweet romantic dream uninterrupted. Or, it can be understood both in the context of *relationship* and in *passion*.

i. In terms of relationship it means, "Let our love progress and grow until it is matured and fruitful, making a genuinely pleasing relationship – *don't let us go too fast*." In terms of passion it means, "Let our love making continue without interruption until we are both fulfilled. Don't let us start until we can go all the way."

B. The spectacular arrival of the wedding party.

1. (6-8) Solomon's entourage brings the maiden to the wedding.

Who *is* this coming out of the wilderness
Like pillars of smoke,
Perfumed with myrrh and frankincense,
With all the merchant's fragrant powders?
Behold, it *is* Solomon's couch,
***With* sixty valiant men around it,**

Of the valiant of Israel.
They all hold swords,
Being expert in war.
Every man *has* his sword on his thigh
Because of fear in the night.

a. **Who is this coming out of the wilderness**: The immediate impression upon reading this is to think that this is the beloved (Solomon) making a dramatic appearance. Yet the ancient Hebrew word translated **this** is in the feminine singular; the question "**Who is this?**" is properly answered, "It is the maiden arriving in Solomon's *palanquin*, for the wedding described at the end of the chapter."

i. Kinlaw explains that the word translated "**this**" is in the feminine singular, and believes it refers to the maiden herself. "It is obviously a wedding procession...our picture is of the groom and his men bringing his bride from her home to his city for the wedding." (Kinlaw)

ii. The other times this question is asked (Who is this?) in Song of Solomon, the answer is the "the maiden" (see Song of Solomon 6:10 and 8:5). "In either case it cannot be Solomon (or the 'king') who is described." (Carr)

iii. Notably, she came **out of the wilderness**, "From whence we little expected to see so beautiful and glorious bride to come, such persons being usually bred in courts or noble cities." (Poole)

iv. "And, doubtless, whenever God shall be pleased to bring forth his Church in power, and to make her mighty among the sons of men, the ignorance of men will be discovered breaking forth in yonder, for they will say, 'Who is this?'" (Spurgeon)

b. **Like pillars of smoke, perfumed**: This adds to the idea of the dignity and impressive character of Solomon's entourage, which was then given to the maiden to bring her to her wedding. She seems to rejoice in this, and happily describes the group as they arrive, complete with **the valiant of Israel**.

i. The apocryphal, inter-testament book 1 Maccabees described a similar wedding party: "Where they lifted up their eyes, and looked, and, behold, there was much ado and great carriage: and the bridegroom came forth, and his friends and brethren, to meet them with drums, and instruments of music, and many weapons." (1 Maccabees 9:39).

ii. This whole procession was *very* impressive. It even was filled with sacred and sacrificial significance, indicated by the description "**perfumed with myrrh and frankincense**." "Although this form occurs only here, the word occurs elsewhere about 115 times with the meaning 'go up in smoke' or 'make (a sacrifice) go up in smoke'." (Carr) The idea is that the smell of **myrrh and frankincense** comes from their burning in a sacrificial sense, as an offering of incense.

iii. **Solomon's couch** uses a different word than in Song of Solomon 3:1, and does not have a sexual connotation.

iv. "There is no reason though why [**this**] should not be read as it normally is and refer to the maiden. If so, we have the scene where the groom has sent for his bride, and she comes properly perfumed in a magnificently appropriate carriage and with an impressive array of protecting attendants." (Kinlaw)

c. **Sixty valiant men around it**: We might say that Solomon's wedding party had **sixty** groomsmen. They weren't there to keep Solomon from backing out of the wedding; they were there to show that he was a powerful man who could genuinely *protect* his maiden.

i. "Of course when travelling through a wilderness, a royal procession was always in danger of attack. Arabs prowled around; wandering Bedouins were always prepared to fall upon the caravan; and more especially was this the case with a marriage procession, because then the robbers might expect to obtain many jewels, or, if not, a heavy ransom for the redemption of the bride or bridegroom by their friends." (Spurgeon)

ii. Therefore the maiden had no need to worry in the **fear of the night**; because she was becoming one with her beloved, what belonged to him now also belonged to her. This expresses the oneness of life and the shared life that should exist between husband and wife. "She and Solomon were so identified with each other at this state that there was a perfect oneness between them. What was his, was hers. What he enjoyed, she enjoyed. This is union." (Nee)

iii. "The very air is perfumed by the smoke of the incense that ascends pillar-like to the clouds; and all that safeguards the position of the Bridegroom Himself, and shows forth His dignity, safeguards also the accompanying bride, the sharer of His glory." (Taylor)

iv. Spurgeon used this text to show that this answers the fears people have about God's church on this earth. "All good men are dead; there are none left to guard the church as before." Yet by symbolic application, the text shows us:

- There are *enough* guards for the church.
- There are *valiant* guards for the church.

- There are guards in the *right places*, all about the church.
- The good guards of the church are *well-armed*, well-trained, always ready, and watchful.

2. (9-11) Solomon enthroned and crowned.

Of the wood of Lebanon
Solomon the King
Made himself a palanquin:
He made its pillars *of* silver,
Its support *of* gold,
Its seat *of* purple,
Its interior paved *with* love
By the daughters of Jerusalem.
Go forth, O daughters of Zion,
And see King Solomon with the crown
With which his mother crowned him
On the day of his wedding,
The day of the gladness of his heart.

a. **Solomon the King made himself a palanquin**: The maiden saw (or imagined herself seeing) herself arriving for her wedding, coming upon the great entourage prepared for Solomon, carried by four or six strong men on a **palanquin**, sort of a portable, ornate couch for carrying an important person.

b. **Pillars of silver...support of gold...seat of purple**: The maiden was impressed not only with the opulence of this **palanquin**, but especially that *he shared all these* symbols of authority and prestige with her. Solomon shared *his best* with his maiden, and Solomon's best was pretty good.

i. It was clear from this that the beloved (Solomon) could do the two essential things a man must be able to do before he is ready to be married: he must be able to *protect* and *provide* for his maiden. The *protection* was shown in the armed men who surrounded this procession; the *provision* was shown in the opulence of Solomon's entourage. Of course, he cannot protect or provide for his maiden (or bride) until he can protect and provide for *himself*; then they live a shared life, a oneness, with whatever belongs to him now also belongs to her also.

ii. This is why a boy must grow up and become a man before he can be a good husband, and why the process of preparing to become a husband and being a husband is good for maturing men. "Love and marriage frequently bring out the noblest qualities in a person. A carefree and somewhat careless young man may become very responsible and diligent. A childish boy may become steady and manly. Why? Because love is the mother of virtue and the father of maturity.... The one you love should bring forth your best qualities and make you a better person." (Glickman)

iii. It also shows that the maiden respected and honored her beloved and saw his strength and authority as a good thing, not a threatening thing – because now it was also, in a sense, *her* strength and authority, because she would be one with him.

c. **See King Solomon with the crown with which his mother crowned him**: When Solomon was anointed and recognized as king – even before the death of his father David – the high priest presided over the ceremony, not his mother Bathsheba (1 Kings 1:38-40). This may mean that the when **his mother crowned him** was when his mother crowned him for his wedding day, in a time of relative innocence when Solomon was captivated by and attached to only one woman.

i. "Not the royal crown used in the coronation/consecration ceremony, but a 'diadem' or 'wreath' made either of branches (like the laurel wreath of the Olympic games), or of precious metals and stones (Psalm 21:3), that is a symbol of honour and joy (*gladness*)." (Carr) This connects well with the rabbinic traditions that a bride and bridegroom were considered to be a "royal couple" on the day of their wedding.

ii. Considering that Solomon had his heart drawn away to *many* women and that these women drew his heart away from God, it is hard to see how this amazing collection of love poems could have come from such a corrupt man. This passage hints at one possible explanation. "Could it be that this is an indication that, if the Song did come from Solomon, it originated before his crowning in his most innocent period?" (Kinlaw)

iii. Yet the mention of **his mother** reminds us of Bathsheba, and the period when she helped Solomon take the throne of Israel (1 Kings 1:11-18; 1:28-31). The connection to 1 Kings 1 brings up the relation between the maiden of the Song of Solomon (called the *Shulamite* in Song of Solomon 6:13) and *Abishag the Shunammite* mentioned in 1 Kings 1:3-4, 1:15, From ancient times, many have wanted to associate the beautiful Abishag with the *Shulamite*. "According to the theory, as she ministered to David, she became romantically involved with his son Solomon and was later the subject of his love poem." (Dilday in commentary on 1 Kings)

iv. Yet we must say that this conjecture at best - and *Shumen* is not the same as *Shulam*. "*Shunem,* the modern Solem, lay eleven kilometers south-east of Nazareth and five kilometers north of Jezreel in Issachar territory, and was visited by Elijah (2 Kings 4:8). There is no need to identify Abishag with the Shulammite of Song of Solomon 6:13." (Wiseman in commentary on 1 Kings)

d. **On the day of his wedding, the day of the gladness of his heart**: It was a glad wedding because their love was real, it was passionate, but it was also pure and restrained into the proper channels. This principle made it a glad day not only for the maiden and the beloved, but also for everyone.

i. "It was not only the day of gladness for the king but also for those who shared in his happiness.... Their love had become a fountain from which all could taste the sweetness of their joy." (Glickman)

Song of Solomon 4 - The Beauty of Consummated Love

A. The beloved praises the appearance and character of the maiden.

1. (1-5) The beloved praises the appearance of the maiden.

Behold, you *are* fair, my love!
Behold, you *are* fair!
You *have* dove's eyes behind your veil.
Your hair *is* like a flock of goats,
Going down from Mount Gilead.
Your teeth *are* like a flock of shorn *sheep*
Which have come up from the washing,
Every one of which bears twins,
And none *is* barren among them.
Your lips *are* like a strand of scarlet,
And your mouth is lovely.
Your temples behind your veil
***Are* like a piece of pomegranate.**
Your neck *is* like the tower of David,
Built for an armory,
On which hang a thousand bucklers,
All shields of mighty men.
Your two breasts *are* like two fawns,
Twins of a gazelle,
Which feed among the lilies.

a. **Behold, you are fair, my love! Behold you are fair**: We may fairly connect this snapshot with the one preceding it, which ended with the wedding procession and ceremony between the maiden and the beloved (Solomon). This section describes the first intimacy of the maiden and the beloved after the wedding and is given to us almost completely in the words of the beloved, who was preparing his maiden for their first experience of marital intimacy.

i. "It was now the night their courtship would end and their marriage begin. The wedding guests had gone. The evening had come...it was an eloquent silence, the silence of anticipation of love fulfilled." (Glickman). Now, the beloved groom was the first to speak and when he spoke he praised the beauty of his bride.

ii. As he spoke, it was evident that the beloved was skilled at showing affection to his maiden. The Apostle Paul would later write, *Let the husband render to his wife the affection due her* (1 Corinthians 7:3). It is wrong for a husband to withhold affection from his wife; and since Paul meant this to apply to every Christian marriage, it shows that *every* wife has affection *due her*. Paul didn't think only the young or pretty or submissive wives were *due* affection; every wife is *due* affection because she is a wife of a Christian man. Jesus is affectionate to His own Bride after the same pattern.

b. **Behold, you are fair, my love! Behold you are fair**: The beloved began not with aggressive or selfish actions, but with tender and confidence building words to his maiden. She had previously doubted her beauty (Song of Solomon 1:5-6); yet he truthfully assured her (doubly so) that she was the most beautiful woman in the world to him.

i. "How sensitive it was of the king to eloquently praise his bride on their wedding night. Even the loveliest girl might feel insecure on this occasion. Yet as always he was sensitive to her and careful to make her secure in his love." (Glickman)

ii. Charles Spurgeon took this as an analogy of how Jesus speaks to and praises His people: "But to hear Christ turn round upon his Church, and seem to say to her 'Thou hast praised me, I will praise thee; thou thinkest much of me, I think quite as much of thee; thou usest great expressions to me, I will use just the same to thee. Thou sayest my love is better than wine, so is thine to me; thou tellest me all my garments smell of myrrh, so do thine; thou sayest my word is sweeter than honey to thy lips, so is thine to mine. All that thou canst say of me, I say it teach to thee; I see myself in thy eyes, I can see my own beauty in thee; and whatever belongs to me, belongs to thee. Therefore, O my love, I will sing back the song: thou hast sung it to thy beloved, and I will sing it to my beloved.'" (Spurgeon)

c. **You have dove's eyes behind your veil**: The beloved not only gave a *general* statement of the maiden's beauty (**Behold, you are fair!**); he also told her specifically how she was beautiful to him. He did this with poetic language more familiar to her ears than to ours, but clearly wanted her to know how beautiful her **eyes** were to him.

i. John Trapp wrote of the characteristics of **dove's eyes**: "Fair, full, clear, chaste." Yet as he took the Song of Solomon to be primarily an allegory, he thought that these beautiful **eyes** belonged to the church, the bride of Christ: "But by 'eyes' here we are chiefly to understand pastors and ministers, those 'seers,' as they were called of old." This is another example of the weakness and danger of an overly-allegorical approach to the Song of Solomon.

ii. This is the first of seven physical features that the beloved described and praised in his maiden (**eyes**, **hair**, **teeth**, **lips**, **temples** and **cheeks**, **neck**, and **breasts**). "In their culture seven was the number of perfection. So even in the number of compliments he gives, the king tells his bride how perfect she is for him." (Glickman)

iii. It also evident that the beloved used his powers of *observation* and *description*; he was focused upon her and not upon himself. Taken with her beauty at the wedding ceremony, he continued the focus into the beauty. He wisely touched her with his words before he touched her with his hands, assuring her that she was captivating and interesting enough to both carefully observe and describe. The maiden could safely yield to a man who cared for her this much, and this unselfishly.

iv. **Behind your veil**: The **veil** was not regular dress for a Jewish woman in Old Testament times. "Normally girls and women wore head-dresses but not veils, except for special occasions. Engagements (Genesis 24:65) and the actual wedding celebration (Genesis 29:23-25) were two of these occasions." (Carr)

d. **Your hair is like a flock of goats**: The idea is not that her hair is like the hair of a goat; rather, it is that her hair beautifully flows down her head like a black-haired **flock of goats, going down from Mount Gilead**. Her hair was long and flowing and seemed to bounce with life.

i. "Most Palestinian goats have long wavy black hair. The movement of a large flock on distant hill makes it appear as if the whole hillside is alive." (Carr)

e. **Your teeth are like a flock of shorn sheep**: The idea isn't that her teeth are wooly; they are like a **flock of shorn sheep** that all look the same, are clean (**come up from the washing**), match one another (**every one of which bears twins**), and are complete (**none is barren among them**).

i. Matthew Poole understood this primarily as an allegory and related it to a description of the church: "By the *teeth* some understand the teachers, which may be compared to teeth, because they prepare, and as it were chew, spiritual food for the people."

f. **Your lips are like a strand of scarlet**: The idea is that her lips are thinner rather than fuller (thought to be more attractive in that day), that they are well outlined, and a beautiful deep red color.

> i. "The delicate outline of a girl's features frequently determines her beauty, especially with respect to her lips. It is this delicate form he praises. With a scarlet threat an artist could perfectly shape a woman's lips." (Glickman)

g. **Your temples behind your veil are like a piece of pomegranate**: The word translated "**temples**" here also includes the cheeks. He saw her **temples** and cheeks as full of color, flushed with both excitement and beauty.

> i. "The term means more broadly 'the side of the face' *i.e.* cheeks." (Carr)

> ii. **A piece of pomegranate** has the idea of the outside of the fruit, not the inside. "The interior of the pomegranate with its juicy red flesh, hard white seeds and yellowish membranes...sounds like a description of an advanced case of acne." (Carr)

h. **Your neck is like the tower of David**: The idea is not that her neck was as long as a tower or proportioned like one. Rather, it speaks of the noble and strong character displayed by her **neck**, both literally and symbolically. In the ancient world, the neck was one part of the body thought to reflect *character*. A bent-over neck was a picture of humiliation. A stiff neck was a sign of stubbornness.

> i. "The tower of David was a military fortress of the nation. The country depended upon the faithfulness and integrity of that fortress. And it must have been very reassuring to loop upon that awesome stronghold, displaying as it did all the shields of war. The people had a healthy respect for it. Therefore, when the king likens the neck of his bride to the fortress, he is paying her a great compliment. The way she carries herself reflects an integrity and character that breeds a healthy respect from all who see her." (Glickman)

i. **Your two breasts are like two fawns...which feed among the lilies**: The idea is that the maiden's breasts look as innocent and attractive as young deer (**fawns**); or also perhaps that her breasts are as beautiful as white fields of lilies marked by the color of **two fawns**.

> i. "A baby deer is soft and gentle, and everyone seeing these little deer long to pet them and play with them. Thus, when the king compares

her breasts to two fawns, he is really saying that he longs to caress her soft and tender breasts." (Glickman)

ii. "It may be the *nipples* especially, which the poet compares to the *two young roes*; and the *lilies* may refer to the *whiteness* of the *breasts* themselves." (Clarke) "The *lilies* being white and swelling, and the *roes* of a reddish colour, and their bodies being hid from sight by the lilies, their heads only appearing above them, bear some resemblance to the red nipples appearing in the top of the lily white breasts.... They are compared to *roes* for their loveliness, of which see Proverbs 5:19; to *young* ones for their smallness, which in breasts is a beauty; to *twins* for their exact likeness." (Poole)

iii. Many commentators follow Trapp's hesitancy to think this refers to the actual **breasts** of an actual woman: "The Church's breasts here are said to be fair, full, and equally matched. Hereby some understand the two testaments.... These breasts are also suitable and equal, as twins."

iv. "The lover's metaphors permit a chasteness and a modesty that less poetic speech would preclude." (Kinlaw)

2. (6) The beloved longs to consummate his love for the maiden.

**Until the day breaks
And the shadows flee away,
I will go my way to the mountain of myrrh
And to the hill of frankincense.**

a. **Until the day breaks and the shadows flee away**: The beloved welcomed the coming of the night, after the celebration of the wedding mentioned in the previous snapshot. Their wedding night was the appropriate setting for the consummation of their deep love.

i. "He will fulfill her request and hence declare that until the light of dawn breaks they will give their love to one another." (Glickman)

b. **I will go my way to the mountain of myrrh and to the hill of frankincense**: Some focus on the **mountain** and **hill** imagery in this verse and believe the beloved longed for the embrace of the maiden's breast. This is possible but doesn't explain well the references to **myrrh** and **frankincense**. It is perhaps better to see this as a poetic reference to their seclusion, surrounded by the luxury and sensual pleasure of rich scents.

3. (7-8) The beloved praises the character of the maiden and tells of his desire to be with her.

**You *are* all fair, my love,
And *there is* no spot in you.**

Come with me from Lebanon, *my* spouse,
With me from Lebanon.
Look from the top of Amana,
From the top of Senir and Hermon,
From the lions' dens,
From the mountains of the leopards.

a. **You are all fair, my love and there is no spot in you**: After giving a seven-fold description of his maiden's beauty, the beloved summarizes his observations. She was more than **fair**; she was **all fair**, and there was **no spot in** her.

i. **No spot in you**: "The word is used only eighteen times in the Old Testament...generally in describing the perfect sacrificial animals which were required." (Carr)

b. **Come with me from Lebanon, my spouse**: Since the maiden came from the north, the beloved poetically invited her to leave the northern region, to leave her family and her fears (alluded to with **lion's dens** and **leopards**) – and to "**come with me**."

i. Before he asked her to pledge the sharing of her virginity, he pledged the sharing of his *life*. "The 'come with me' of our translation is in Hebrew *itti* ('with me') twice repeated, a prepositional phrase used as an invitation! He wants her with him. 'With me' sums up his desire." (Kinlaw)

ii. This is the first time he calls the maiden his **spouse**, his bride – and then he uses the word repeatedly. According to Kinlaw, it could very well be that the Hebrew word for **spouse** (*bride*) comes from the root *to complete*.

iii. **Spouse**: "The focus of the word is on the married status of the woman, particularly on the sexual element presupposed in that status as 'the completed one.'" (Carr)

iv. **From the lions' dens, from the mountains of the leopards**: "In asking her to come from such fearful places, he is really asking her to bring her thoughts completely to him and leave her fears behind and perhaps to leave the lingering thoughts of home behind as well...he wished her to leave her fear and anxiety about the new life of marriage and simply come to him.... So he calls her from her fears to his arms." (Glickman)

4. (9-11) The beloved expresses the depth of his passion for the maiden.

You have ravished my heart,
My sister, *my* spouse;

You have ravished my heart
With one *look* of your eyes,
With one link of your necklace.
How fair is your love,
My sister, *my* spouse!
How much better than wine is your love,
And the scent of your perfumes
Than all spices!
Your lips, O *my* spouse,
Drip as the honeycomb;
Honey and milk *are* under your tongue;
And the fragrance of your garments
Is like the fragrance of Lebanon.

a. **You have ravished my heart, my sister, my spouse**: Here the beloved went beyond praising the maiden's beauty and even character; he described the *effect* that she had upon him. **With one look of your eyes**, he was a changed man and deeply in love with her.

i. **You have ravished my heart**: "'Thou hast hearted me,' i.e., taken away my heart." (Clarke)

ii. **Sister**: "At last she would become his wife...that is the reason he calls her his sister. In their culture 'sister' was an affectionate term for one's wife." (Glickman)

iii. "*My sister*, so he calls her, partly because both he and she had one and the same father, to wit, God...and partly to show the greatness of his love to her, which is such as cannot be sufficiently expressed by any one relation, but must borrow the perfections and affections of all to describe it." (Poole)

iv. "As if he could not express his near and dear relationship to her by any one term, he employs the two. 'My sister' – that is, one by birth, partaker of the same nature. 'My spouse' – that is, one in love, joined by sacred ties of affection that never can be snapped. 'My sister' by birth, 'My spouse' by choice. 'My sister' in communion, 'My spouse' in absolute union with myself." (Spurgeon)

b. **How fair is your love.... How much better than wine is your love**: The beloved's praise of the maiden's love reminds us that she was not a passive recipient of his love. He initiated the relationship and pursued her; but she responded with beautiful and precious love all her own.

i. **How much better than wine is your love**: "This same she had said of him in Song of Solomon 1:2. Now he returns it upon her, as is usual among lovers." (Trapp) Spurgeon applied this principle to the relationship between Jesus and His people: "Now can you believe it? Just what you think of Christ's love, Christ thinks of yours. You value his love, and you are right in so doing; but I am afraid that still you undervalue it. He even values your love, if I may so speak, he sets a far higher estimate upon it than you do; he thinks very much of little, he estimates it not by its strength, but by its sincerity." (Spurgeon)

ii. This compliment showed she wasn't passive in their lovemaking. "He found her not lovely only, but loving; he had made her so, and now takes singular delight and complacency in his own work." (Trapp)

iii. **And the scent of your perfumes than all spices!** "The sense of the colon is not that her *perfumes* are better than any others, but that to her lover even her everyday anointing oils smell better than the most exotic perfumes." (Carr)

c. **Your lips, O my spouse...honey and milk are under your tongue**: The beloved described the sweetness of the kisses of the maiden.

i. "Way back then the king tells his bride that honey and milk are under her tongue. But this expression may tell us more than that French kissing was around long before the French." (Glickman)

d. **The fragrance of your garments**: The whole scene is intimate and filled with beautiful sights, smells, tastes, and words. We are poetically and tastefully brought to the point of the consummation of their intimacy.

i. "*Garments* is not the common word for clothing.... The *salma* is the outer garment which served both as a cloak for the day and a cover while sleeping. This latter usage gave rise to the use of the word for a bed-covering.... In the context here, some sort of sleep-wear (negligee?) may be implied." (Carr)

B. The consummation of the love between the maiden and the beloved.

1. (12-15) The beloved praises the virginity of the maiden.

A garden enclosed
***Is* my sister, *my* spouse,**
A spring shut up,
A fountain sealed.
Your plants *are* an orchard of pomegranates
With pleasant fruits,
Fragrant henna with spikenard,
Spikenard and saffron,
Calamus and cinnamon,
With all trees of frankincense,

Myrrh and aloes,
With all the chief spices—
A fountain of gardens,
A well of living waters,
And streams from Lebanon.

a. **A garden enclosed is my sister, my spouse, a spring shut up, a fountain sealed**: With these three images the beloved praised the virginity of his maiden and did so immediately before receiving the gift of her virginity. Her sexuality had not been given to another; it was like an **enclosed garden**, a protected **spring**, a **fountain sealed**.

i. **A garden**: "A garden is neither common ground nor ground for the planting of things at random, nor is it ground for mere agricultural purposes, but for the production of something for beauty and pleasure." (Nee)

- The idea of this garden suggests *privacy*; the maiden's sexuality was to be privately expressed.

- The idea of this garden suggests *separation*; the maiden's sexuality was to be focused on and set apart to her beloved. "A garden indeed, but she was not a public garden." (Nee)

- The idea of this garden suggests *sacredness*; the maiden's sexuality was something holy, and both she and the beloved were to regard it as such.

- The idea of this garden suggests *security*; the maiden's sexuality was to be respected and not violated, even by the beloved – it was only to be expressed in the context of security.

ii. **A spring shut up, a fountain sealed**: The idea is not that this metaphorical **spring** or **fountain** is dried up and useless; rather that it is protected so that its water can only go to its rightful owner. "To 'seal' a spring was to enclose it and protect the water for its rightful owner; Hezekiah did this when he had the tunnel dug from the Virgin's Spring at Gihon to the Pool of Siloam to safeguard Jerusalem's water supply [2 Kings 20:20]." (Carr)

iii. The beloved therefore recognized the *great value* of the maiden's virginity, as she also recognized. Individuals and societies suffer greatly when virginity is no longer valued. It is important for parents, young men, young women, and the church as a whole to value virginity and never treat it as something to be embarrassed of. In addition, the concept of a restored or a "from-now-on" virginity should be promoted and valued.

iv. Seeing the high value of virginity also helps us to understand the Biblical commands against pre-marital sex. It is helpful to refute many myths about pre-marital sex:

- *Myth: "The Bible says nothing against premarital sex."* Fact: The high value placed on virginity, seen here and in other passages such as Deuteronomy 22:13-29 shows premarital sex is wrong. But it also clearly found in the passages that speak against the sexual sin known in the New Testament as *porneia*, and commonly translated "fornication" (1 Corinthians 6:13 and 6:18; Ephesians 5:3 and 5:5; 1 Thessalonians 4:3. *Porneia* broadly refers to all types of sexual activity outside of marriage (including homosexuality); it encompasses practically all sexual behavior outside of that which is practiced between a husband and a wife in the bonds of their marriage.

- *Myth: "He wants to have sex with me because he loves me."* Fact: His love for you will be proved by his willingness to wait for marriage. The desire for sex does not prove love in a man. In one survey, 55% of men said "yes" to the following question: "If you could be certain that your wife or girlfriend would never know, would you have sex with any of her friends?" And to the question, "Have you ever had sex with a woman you have actively disliked?" 58% of men said "yes". *You are foolish if you think a boy loves you - or even likes you - because he wants to have sex with you.*

- *Myth: "My boyfriend is a Christian and loves the Lord. I don't have to worry about that."* Fact: Christian men face the same challenges as non-Christians when it comes to sexual desires and lusts. They have the *ability* to overcome those lusts by the power of the Holy Spirit, but it isn't easy and many who thought they were strong enough have fallen to these sins.

- *Myth: "We are going to get married, so it doesn't matter."* Fact: It does matter. First, you are setting a value on your own sexuality; there is a sense in which a woman then gives her future husband the right to treat her as an object. Second, you are setting a pattern; you are agreeing that in some circumstances, sex outside of marriage is acceptable, and this is something you don't want in your mind or in the mind of your marriage partner; especially because on of the most important aspects of a long lasting, fulfilling sexual relationship is *trust*. Third, you are only taking *away* from the blessing God intends for your sexual relationship when married.

- *Myth: "We can be married before God."* Fact: If you were on a desert island without any intuitions of government or society, this might be an argument. But marriage in both the Biblical and cultural sense is being joined together in a public ceremony that is recognized as legal and legitimate by the law and the culture. You aren't on a desert island.

b. **Your plants are an orchard of pomegranates with pleasant fruits, fragrant henna with spikenard**: Since he introduced the metaphor of a **garden**, the beloved poetically described the value and beauty of the maiden's sexuality.

i. Some take the metaphor of the **garden** to be a rather direct reference to the female genitalia. Given the continued metaphorical description of these verses, it is better to see the **garden** more as a reference to the maiden's sexuality in general. Of course, this idea is connected to her anatomy, but its concept is less direct.

c. **A fountain of gardens, a well of living waters**: The images reinforce the idea of richness and abundance. The beloved understood that the maiden's virginity was not previously spent because it was considered small and insignificant; rather it was protected because it was great and important. Now that her virginity would be properly yielded, its abundant and life-giving character would be seen and experienced.

i. As stated before, the expression of the maiden's sexuality was to be private, separate, sacred, and secure. Yet the goodness and benefit of such a godly expression of sexuality would benefit her whole person, and that benefit would be *public*, like **a fountain of gardens, a well of living waters**.

ii. "Her garden is a paradise of delightful fruits, fragrant flowers, colorful blossoms, towering trees and aromatic spices. She is overwhelmingly beautiful, as refreshing and uplifting as spring flowers and enchanting spices. She was the embodiment of the rich life of spring itself." (Glickman)

iii. In seeing the goodness and honor and blessing of virginity – of a woman's sexuality being protected and not trampled upon until it is ready to be properly yielded in marriage – it is almost impossible for those women who have not properly guarded their virginity (or worse yet had it stolen from them) to feel that they can never enjoy this blessing or anything like it. It is true that once entered, this garden can no longer be un-entered. But to extend the garden metaphor, a garden that has been trodden upon and is in disarray can be restored again to health and beauty through wisdom, self-control, effort, and most importantly through the work of the Master Gardener (the one who created the woman's sexuality). It cannot be un-entered if it already has been, but it can be restored to goodness.

iv. These principles apply equally unto men, who may of course also unwisely forfeit their virginity. Like the woman taken in adultery and brought before Jesus, one can hear the words from their Savior, "Neither do I condemn You" and "Go and sin no more."

2. (16) The maiden yields her virginity to her beloved.

Awake, O north *wind*,
And come, O south!
Blow upon my garden,
***That* its spices may flow out.**
Let my beloved come to his garden
And eat its pleasant fruits.

a. **Awake, O north wind, and come O south! Blow upon my garden**: Here, for the first and only time in this section, the maiden speaks. First, she took the **garden** imagery introduced by her beloved, and thought of gentle winds releasing and carrying the fragrance of a literal garden. In this she asked both her beloved (and perhaps also her God) to release the beautiful fragrance of her preserved, protected sexuality – now ready to be yielded to her beloved.

i. "As the breezes of spring are the fragrant messengers of a garden sent to lure the outside world within, so now she requests those breezes to blow upon her garden and bring her lover to her.... With poetic beauty and propriety she asks her lover to possess her." (Glickman)

b. **Let my beloved come to his garden and eat its pleasant fruits**: *This* is the moment of yielded virginity, where the beloved is invited to enjoy the previously protected and sealed sexuality of the maiden. A line before, the maiden called it "**my garden**"; now it was **his garden**. Her virginity, her sexuality, was protected so that it could be fully given to her **beloved**.

i. "And she calls the garden both *hers* and *his*, because of the oneness which is between them...whereby they have a common interest one in another's person and concerns." (Poole)

ii. The *description* is poetic and shy; the *experience* was deep and moving.

iii. He and he alone has the right to **eat** the **pleasant fruits** of her garden; only he can enjoy the pleasure and blessing of the maiden's sexuality.

iv. Some who take the **garden** metaphor as a direct reference to female genitalia believe this describes a specific sex act that the beloved performed upon the woman, involving the lips of the beloved and the metaphorical **garden** of the maiden. This is an unnecessary over-interpretation of this passage, though such acts are entirely permissible for non-coerced, fully consenting married couples under the principle of the honorable and undefiled marriage bed of Hebrews 13:4.

v. Taking these lines as allegorical and applying them to the life of the believer with their Savior, G. Campbell Morgan wrote: "The one overwhelming passion of the loved of the Lord, is to give His heart satisfaction, to provide from Him the precious fruits for which He in love is seeking. That we may do that, we call for the north wind and for the south; for adversity and prosperity; for winter and summer; in order that by their varied ministries, we may become to Him a garden of delights."

3. (5:1a) The beloved receives the offered virginity of the maiden.

I have come to my garden, my sister, *my* spouse;
I have gathered my myrrh with my spice;
I have eaten my honeycomb with my honey;
I have drunk my wine with my milk.

a. **I have come to my garden, my sister, my spouse**: The beloved accepted the invitation of his maiden and had received her virginity as a precious gift. The long anticipated, passionate desires were now rightly and beautifully consummated.

i. "Here, for the first time in the Song, the 'garden' is opened and entrance is invited and fulfilled." (Carr)

ii. "The language used here of love's consummation is classic in its chasteness, a character possible only through the use of symbolic language.... Metaphor plays the same role here as the veil in the temple. Sinful man needs such to protect the mystery." (Kinlaw)

b. **My garden**: In the previous verse the maiden made the transition from "my garden" to "his garden." Now the beloved received her gift, and made her **garden** – that is, her sexuality – *his own*. There was a very real sense in which her sexuality now belonged to him (and his to her).

i. The Apostle Paul reinforced this principle in his first letter to the Corinthians: *The wife does not have authority over her own body, but the husband does. And likewise the husband does not have authority over his own body, but the wife does.* (1 Corinthians 7:4)

ii. Of course, this principle could never justify a husband abusing or coercing his wife, sexually or otherwise. Paul's point was that we have a *binding obligation* to serve our marriage partner with physical affection. It is an awesome obligation: out of the billions of people on the earth, God has chosen *one*, and *one alone*, to meet our sexual needs. There is to be no one else.

c. **I have gathered my myrrh with my spice...honeycomb...honey... wine...milk**: Using the images of luxury and satisfaction, the beloved poetically described how pleasing their experience of intimacy was.

i. "So few couples seem to experience that kind of wedding night. Why is this so? Perhaps one reason is that their courtship does not prepare them for it." (Glickman)

4. (5:1b) The comment from heaven.

Eat, O friends!
Drink, yes, drink deeply,
O beloved ones!

a. **Eat, O friends! Drink, yes, drink deeply**: There is considerable disagreement among commentators as to who speaks these words. Some believe that the groom left the marriage bedroom and spoke to the remaining guests of the wedding party. Others think of an imaginary chorus, such as the previously mentioned *Daughters of Jerusalem*. On balance, it is best to see these words as divine; an approving statement from heaven, glorying in the goodness and purity of their love.

i. Adam Clarke describes the idea that this was addressed to guests at the wedding party: "These are generally supposed to be the words of the *bridegroom*, after he returned from the *nuptial chamber*, and exhibited those *signs* of his wife's *purity* which the customs of those times required. This being a cause of universal joy, the entertainment is served up; and he invites his companions, and the friends of both parties, to eat and drink abundantly, as there was such a universal cause of rejoicing." (Clarke)

b. **O beloved ones**: This was the best of relationships. Not only were the marriage couple deeply in love, but they also were **beloved** of God. We might say that no one was more pleased over their relationship than God Himself. This was the beginning of a *blessed* sexual relationship.

i. "He lifts his voice and gives hearty approval to the entire night. He vigorously endorses and affirms the love of this couple. He takes pleasure in what has taken place." (Glickman)

Song of Solomon 5 - The Maiden's Dream

A. The maiden describes her dream.

1. (2) The maiden dreams of her beloved coming to her door at night.

I sleep, but my heart is awake;
It is **the voice of my beloved!**
He knocks, *saying,*
"Open for me, my sister, my love,
My dove, my perfect one;
For my head is covered with dew,
My locks with the drops of the night."

a. **I sleep, but my heart is awake**: In this poetic snapshot, the maiden described another dream-like experience. The maiden is described as being either asleep, yet dreaming, or in the twilight of almost-sleep where one is not quite sure if they are awake or asleep.

b. **It is the voice of my beloved**: In her half-awake, half-asleep state the maiden heard the **voice of** her **beloved** outside her door. He had come, either for an unexpected rendezvous or after a long day of looking after his responsibilities.

c. **He knocks, saying, "Open for me, my sister, my love"**: Having come in some way unexpectedly (perhaps *later* than expected), the beloved found himself locked outside the maiden's home – which, presumably, was also his own home.

i. It isn't really important whether this section should be chronologically arranged after or before the wedding and consummation previously described. The emphasis here is not on the married or non-married status of the leading man and woman, but on a difficulty in their relationship.

d. **My sister, my love, my dove, my perfect one**: First the beloved *called* for his maiden, but the sound of his voice was not enough to persuade

144

her to open the door. Then he *affectionately praised* his maiden, with each of these warm and complimentary terms. Yet this also was not enough to persuade her to open the door.

i. **My sister**: One suggestion with this title is *permanence*. One remains a *sister* forever, and that is how long the beloved wanted to be connected with his maiden.

ii. **My love, my dove**: "The title of *dove* signifies her chastity and constant faithfulness to her Husband, for which doves are famous." (Poole)

iii. **My perfect one**: "The AV *undefiled* suggests 'virgin', but that connotation is absent from the Hebrew. Ethical and moral blamelessness is more the idea." (Carr)

e. **For my head is covered with dew**: The final appeal of the beloved was a description of the discomforts he had endured in seeking after the maiden. Like a shepherd out late at night watching over the flocks, his head was wet with the moisture of the **dew** that covered the land that night.

i. "He alludes to the custom of lovers, which oft and willingly suffer such inconveniences for their hopes and desires of enjoying their beloved." (Poole)

ii. The beloved made several appeals to the maiden:

- *The appeal of his presence*; simply knowing that he sought her out and was at the door might have persuaded the maiden to open the door.

- *The voice of the beloved*; the sound of his call to her should have prompted her to open the door.

- *The specific request*; when the beloved asked, "**Open for me**," it should have been enough to make the maiden open the door.

- *The warm and affectionate appeal*; the tender and beautiful names that he called the maiden should have melted her heart. Nowhere else in the song does he pour out upon her so many affectionate names.

- *The description of his own discomforts for her sake*; if nothing else, these should have warmed her heart to open the door.

iii. Yet for all this, the maiden did not open the door for the beloved and allow him to enter in!

iv. This picture – of the beloved standing outside the door and appealing to his maiden for entry – may provide the only New Testament reference to the Song of Solomon, found at Revelation 3:20: *Behold, I stand at the door and knock. If anyone hears My voice and opens the door, I will come in to him and dine with him, and he with Me.*

2. (3-6) The maiden fails to meet her beloved at the door.

I have taken off my robe;
How can I put it on *again?*
I have washed my feet;
How can I defile them?
My beloved put his hand
By the latch *of the door,*
And my heart yearned for him.
I arose to open for my beloved,
And my hands dripped *with* **myrrh,**
My fingers with liquid myrrh,
On the handles of the lock.
I opened for my beloved,
But my beloved had turned away *and* **was gone.**
My heart leaped up when he spoke.
I sought him, but I could not find him;
I called him, but he gave me no answer.

a. **I have taken off my robe; how can I put it on again**: In response to the warm appeal of the beloved, the maiden answered only with excuses. She was comfortable in her bed, so he could not come in. She could not be bothered with the inconvenience of dressing herself and preparing herself for sleep again (**I have washed my feet; how can I defile them?**).

i. **How can I**: "Often it is found in songs of mourning or lamentation, and here reflects a petulant unwillingness to act rather than the impossibility of action...she appears unwilling to put herself to any trouble even for her lover." (Carr)

ii. **My robe**: "It is the garment worn next to the skin, not the 'garment' of Song of Solomon 4:11 which served as a bed-covering, nor the common *begged* which was used to described clothing in general. Delitzsch's comment 'she lies unclothed in bed', catches the precise meaning of the colon." (Carr)

iii. Perhaps she was simply not willing to be inconvenienced; perhaps she did not appreciate the unexpected nature of the beloved's visit; perhaps he came much later than she had expected him, and therefore she felt annoyed. Perhaps this was her effort to control the relationship ("Why should I run as soon as he knocks? He can wait a little while.")

Whatever the specific reason, she refused to promptly rise from bed and open the door.

iv. Her problem was not that she didn't go to the door; but that she did it so slowly and reluctantly, making excuses all along the way. "This attitude shows an insensitive spirit. She was thinking only about her comfort and not at all about Solomon's desires or her relationship with him." (Estes)

v. "This is a remarkable picture of the kind of adjustments that are necessary in life style in marriage. Our natural sloth, the differences between a man and a woman, our uncertainty about the other's thinking, the variations in our life rhythms, our unwillingness to alter our preferred patterns for the other, our own self-consciousness – all contribute to the problem of reading each other's advances." (Kinlaw)

vi. "Although this romance is an ideal, it is not a fantasy. It is realistic, and presents the realistic problems of marriage...also the principles for solving them." (Glickman)

b. **My beloved put his hand by the latch of the door**: The maiden could hear that the **beloved** put his hand upon the latch mechanism of the door. This was a clear (and final) indication of his desire to enter and be with her, *but only at her invitation*. The beloved would not break or force the **latch** of the door but insisted that the way be opened to him.

i. Some commentators and translators have wondered if the wording here presents a *double entendre*, cleverly describing sexual intercourse between the beloved and the maiden. The basis for this is found in the fact that on at least one occasion (Isaiah 57:8) in the Old Testament, this Hebrew word translated **hand** is a euphemism for the male sexual organ. In addition, the word translated **latch of the door** is more literally "opening" or "hole."

ii. The idea behind this *double entendre* is better illustrated by comparing some other translations of the phrase:

- NIV: *My lover thrust his hand through the latch-opening.*
- NASB: *My beloved extended his hand through the opening.*
- LXX: *My kinsman put forth his hand by the hole of the door.*
- KJV: *My beloved put in his hand by the hole of the door.*
- NLT: *My lover tried to unlatch the door.*

iii. While allowing for the slight possibility of such a *double entendre*, it clearly is not the direct meaning of the section, as demonstrated by the context. The idea of the couple engaged in intercourse does not match the context, which places the beloved as *outside* the presence of the maiden, which is the dynamic that drives the entire section. If anything, the *double entendre* may refer to the conflicted sexual longings within the maiden (especially with the phrase, **my heart yearned for him**). She obviously loved and longed for her beloved yet refused to promptly open the door for him.

iv. "If it were a *real scene*, which is mentioned in this and the two following verses, it must refer, from the well-known use of the *metaphors*, to matrimonial endearments. Or, it may refer to his *attempts to open the door*, when she hesitated to arise, on the grounds mentioned. But this also bears every evidence of a *dream*." (Clarke)

v. "None of this is decisive, of course, but as Cook notes, the *double entendre* by nature is 'so delicate as to leave some doubt about its presence at a specific point'. Nevertheless, this appears to be one text where the erotic meaning is present. If *yad* does mean the male member here, *hor* is its female counterpart." (Carr)

c. **I arose to open for my beloved**: It wasn't that the maiden *refused* to open for her **beloved**; it was that she long delayed to do so, and delayed out of self-interest and self-indulgence, probably connected with some resentment towards the beloved.

i. Here the writer gave us an emotionally accurate picture of the dynamic of conflict in a relationship, especially in marriage.

- The maiden felt resentment towards the beloved (the nature and reasonableness of that resentment is impossible to determine).

- The beloved refused to force himself upon his maiden and would only enter at her invitation.

- The beloved made a true and persistent appeal to his maiden, that they might be together and enjoy their relationship.

- Because of her resentment, the maiden long delayed her response to the desire of the beloved.

- When she finally did respond, it seemed too late – the moment had passed, and her beloved was gone.

ii. In applying this dynamic of conflict to a relationship, one may fairly reverse the roles of maiden/beloved and wife/husband, but the fundamental principles remain. Significant damage may be done to a relationship by:

- Holding on to resentments and refusing to be generous with forgiveness.

- The attempt to force one's interest and affections upon another, and not waiting for their response.

- Refusing or delaying response when approached in a loving and persistent way.

- Failing to appreciate the value of an appeal to resume or build relationship, typically out of self-interest and self-indulgence, or a desire to control the relationship.

d. **And my hands dripped with myrrh**: As the maiden finally rose from bed and came to the door, she noticed that the door or the latch of the door had been anointed with sweet perfume. This was another reminder of the beauty and the quality of his love for her.

i. According to Clarke, it was a custom among some ancient peoples to anoint doors used by a bride with fragrant oils, and this same custom (or some form of it) may have existed among the ancient Jews. (Clarke)

ii. "He simply left her a 'love note' and then went away. In their culture a lover would leave this fragrant myrrh at the door as a sign that he had been there." (Glickman)

iii. His response – not of anger, not of objection, but simply a non-threatening display of love – would soon awaken a loving response in her. This is a wonderful picture of the way a husband should respond when he feels disrespected by his wife; instead of angrily demanding respect, he should instead display his love for her in a non-threatening way and wait for the response of love to her.

e. **I opened for my beloved, but my beloved had turned away and was gone**: When the maiden finally came to the door – shaking off her previous self-indulgence, laziness, and perhaps desire to control the relationship – she found that her beloved **was gone**. She was too late.

i. "The presence and comfort of her Bridegroom are again lost to her; not this time by relapse into worldliness, but by slothful self-indulgence.... And more than this, the door of her chamber was not only closed, but barred; an evidence that His return was neither eagerly desired nor expected." (Taylor)

f. **I called him, but he gave me no answer**: Now the roles were reversed. Where once the beloved called for the maiden and heard no response, now the maiden calls for him but hears **no answer**. She had foolishly waited too long to respond, actually working against her own self-interest.

i. If we consider this all happening, it lends to the idea that this is in fact a dream sequence of the maiden. In the sense of the text, it does not seem that she lingered so long that when she did open the door it was too late to see where he went. Yet in the creative nature of dreams, it is entirely natural. In whatever sense dreams make, the slowness of her response was directly connected to her difficulty in finding him.

3. (7-8) The maiden's disappointing search for her beloved.

The watchmen who went about the city found me.
They struck me, they wounded me;
The keepers of the walls
Took my veil away from me.
I charge you, O daughters of Jerusalem,
If you find my beloved,
That you tell him I *am* lovesick!

a. **The watchmen who went about the city found me. They struck me, they wounded me**: In her dream, the maiden sought and called for her beloved (Song of Solomon 5:6), extending her search to the streets of the **city**. This ended only in disappointment, because she did not find her beloved, nor did she find any help from **the watchmen** or from **the keepers of the walls**.

i. Since this happened in a dream and not in reality, this may reflect the maiden's guilt over her previous response to him (or lack thereof). Kinlaw asks this question: "Does this treatment by the watchmen reflect the girl's guilt and sense of failure at the slowness of her response to her husband?"

b. **The keepers of the walls took my veil away from me**: In her dream, not only was the maiden unsuccessful, but those who did not sympathize enough with her search also mistreated her.

i. This **veil** is probably better understood as a scarf or mantle; it is a distinctly different article of clothing mentioned in Song of Solomon 1:7, 4:3, 4:11, and 5:3.

c. **Tell him I am lovesick**: The maiden's plea to the **daughters of Jerusalem** shows that she came to regret and suffer under her previous actions. Now she was **lovesick**, but not at all in same sense as previously mentioned in Song of Solomon 2:5. Previously she was overwhelmed by the presence of love; here she was aching at its absence.

i. "There is a realism in the Song that merits our respect. The course of true love seldom runs smoothly for long. For every moment of ecstasy, there seems to be the moment of hurt and pain." (Kinlaw)

ii. By application to spiritual life, we may say that there are some sicknesses that are unique to the saints:

- Sin-sickness, when the soul hates sin and wants nothing to do with it.
- Self-sickness, when the soul comes to hate self-indulgence, self-seeking, self-exalting, and self-reliance of every sort.
- Love-sickness of the first type, when the believer is so deeply moved by the love of God that they feel they can hardly bear it.
- Love-sickness of the second type, when the believer feels distanced from or deserted by Jesus, and longs for a renewed sense of closeness.

iii. Spurgeon described this second type of lovesickness in this way: "It is the longing of a soul, then, not for salvation, and not even for the certainty of salvation, but for the enjoyment of present fellowship with him who is her soul's life, her soul's all.... It is a panting after communion." (Spurgeon)

B. The maiden describes her beloved.

1. (9) The Daughters of Jerusalem ask about the beloved.

What *is* your beloved
More than *another* beloved,
O fairest among women?
What *is* your beloved
More than *another* beloved,
That you so charge us?

a. **What is your beloved more than another beloved**: The dream-sequence request to the daughters of Jerusalem in the previous verse (Song of Solomon 5:8) now had a response. In essence, the daughters of Jerusalem wanted to know what was so special about the maiden's **beloved**. They wanted an explanation as for why she was so *lovesick* (Song of Solomon 5:8) and why she so desperately sought him.

i. "Her anguish at her loss was so extreme, her heart-sickness was so agonizing, her frenzy so bewildering, that they were startled into feeling that he of whom she was bereft was no common lover." (Meyer)

b. **O fairest among women**: This may have been spoken sarcastically, because (in her dream) the maiden's appearance may have been neglected by her rapid rising, her frantic search, and her mistreatment by the watchmen (Song of Solomon 5:7).

2. (10-16) The maiden responds by describing the beloved.

My beloved *is* white and ruddy,
Chief among ten thousand.

His head *is like* the finest gold;
His locks *are* wavy,
And black as a raven.
His eyes *are* like doves
By the rivers of waters,
Washed with milk,
And fitly set.
His cheeks *are* like a bed of spices,
Banks of scented herbs.
His lips *are* lilies,
Dripping liquid myrrh.
His hands *are* rods of gold
Set with beryl.
His body *is* carved ivory
Inlaid *with* sapphires.
His legs *are* pillars of marble
Set on bases of fine gold.
His countenance *is* like Lebanon,
Excellent as the cedars.
His mouth *is* most sweet,
Yes, he *is* altogether lovely.
This *is* my beloved,
And this *is* my friend,
O daughters of Jerusalem!

a. **My beloved is**: With this, the maiden began an extended description of her **beloved**, somewhat answering to his description of her in Song of Solomon 4:1-7. It showed the she could be as eloquent in describing him as he was in describing her.

i. "Love songs describing the physical beauty of the beloved are common in the ancient Near East, but most of them describe the female. Such detailed description of the male, as here, is seldom recorded." (Carr)

ii. The description uses many figures of speech and expressions that sound strange to us, but the main idea is unmistakable. She was attracted to her beloved both by his character and by his physical appearance. "Here she may seem to speak with the tongues of men and of angels, performing, as lovers used to do, that for him that he had done for her before." (Trapp)

iii. "Instead of thinking of herself, she started thinking of her beloved. Instead of wanting her comfort and convenience, she desired to nurture the relationships she had started to take for granted." (Estes)

iv. Curiously, in the context of her dream, she did not say these things to her beloved, but she said these things *about* him in the presence of others. It was more important for *her* to be convinced of these things than it was for *him* to hear them.

b. **My beloved is white and ruddy, chief among then thousand**: Here she described both his countenance (**white and ruddy**) and his greatness (**chief among ten thousand**). She loved him not only for who he was to her, but also for the greatness of his character and accomplishments.

i. **Ruddy**: "Most commentators take this simply as the normal complexion of a healthy young man." According to Carr, the ancient Hebrew word is *adom*, and Carr says: "The Hebrew noun *adam*, 'man', is a more likely source for the term here, in which case, her lover is 'manly'."

ii. This admiration of a man's greatness is a strong motivator for accomplishment among men. A man very much wants his wife to recognize whatever greatness or accomplishments he has attained.

iii. "The metaphors are ancient Near Eastern ones, but the import is clear: he is one in ten thousand." (Kinlaw)

c. **His head is like the finest gold; his locks are wavy**: The maiden saw her beloved as radiant and attractive, from beginning with his head and continuing down in her description of his appearance. His **head is like the finest gold**, with the idea that his face is well-proportioned and colored, with the idea of quality and prestige.

d. **His eyes are like doves by the rivers of waters.... His cheeks are like a bed of spices.... His hands are rods of gold.... His countenance is like Lebanon, as excellent as the cedars**: The description is of a man who is more than attractive, but also strong and of great character.

i. **Washed with milk, and fitly set**: "The sense appears to be describing the contrast of the iris with the white of the eye, both *fitly set* (NIV *mounted like jewels*) in the face." (Carr)

ii. **His cheeks are like a bed of spices**: "But it has been supposed to refer to his *beard*, which in a *young well-made man* is exceedingly beautiful. I have seen young Turks, who had taken much care of their beards, mustachios, &c., look majestic. Scarcely any thing serves to set off the human face to greater advantage than the *beard*, when kept in proper order. Females admire it in their *suitors* and *husbands*. I have known cases, where they not only *despised* but *execrated* Europeans, whose faces were close shaved. The men perfume their beards often;

and this may be what is intended by *spices* and *sweet-smelling myrrh*." (Clarke)

iii. **His countenance is like Lebanon**: "As Lebanon exalts its head beyond all the other mountains near Jerusalem, so my beloved is tall and majestic, and surpasses in stature and majesty all other men." (Clarke)

iv. Watchman Nee approached this book primarily as an allegory describing the relationship between Jesus and His people. On that basis, he took the features of this description and allegorically applied them to Jesus.

- **White and ruddy**: "The ruddy complexion of perfect health. This indicated that He was vibrant with fullness of life and power."

- **His head is like the finest gold**: "This is a description of His divine attributes. He possessed God's life and God's glory."

- **His locks are wavy, and black as a raven**: "An indication of His everlasting vigor and power."

- **His eyes are like doves**: "Eyes are the seat of expression, and this description also speaks of an intimacy known by the spouse."

- **His cheeks are like a bed of spices, banks of scented herbs**: "These same cheeks had undergone much shame and despite.... No wonder, then, that such a believer as this one looked upon His cheeks as a bed of fragrant spices or scented herbs."

- **His lips are lilies, dripping liquid myrrh**: "The 'lilies' referred to here speak of kingly glory.... How glorious were the teachings of Christ! And how sweet were the words which dropped from His lips!"

- **His hands are rods of gold**: "The strength of His hands to establish firmly and bring to completion the purposes of God."

- **His body is carved ivory**: "The Lord Jesus, too, was a Person rich with the deepest sensibilities, that He was moved with great feelings of love for His people."

- **His legs are pillars of marble**: "They signify His power to stand...as having immovable stability."

- **His countenance is like Lebanon, excellent as the cedars**: "Shows something of His elevated character. Though a Man, yet He was now a Man glorified in the heights of heaven."

- **His mouth is most sweet**: "It speaks of a certain aspect of His mediatorial work."

v. Spurgeon mused on this spiritual analogy, and the importance of the believer considering Jesus: "When you get sick, and sad, and weary of God's people, turn your thoughts to God himself; and if ever you see any spots in the Church, Christ's bride, look at her glorious Husband, and you will only love him the more as you think of his wondrous condescension in having loved such a poor thing as his Church is even at her best." (Spurgeon)

e. **Yes, he is altogether lovely**: She summarized her description with this one general phrase. In her mind, there was something complete and great in his physical appearance and standing as a man.

i. "The force of the whole unit is that in the girl's eyes her lover (be he king or peasant) is beyond comparison." (Carr) He was tall, dark, and handsome; with a tanned face and dark hair, but his eyes were soft and tender. His cologne smelled good and his hands were so strong and gentle that they were as precious as gold. He was strongly built from head to toe and most of all had a dignified bearing.

ii. If we apply this to the relationship between the believer and Jesus Christ, these descriptions give a sense of how greatly the believer prizes their Lord. "But all of these gathered together are poor and unworthy emblems of the peerless beauty of Emmanuel. White in purity, ruddy with the bloodstain, his bushy locks emblematical of immortal youth, his eyes like waterbrooks reflecting the deep azure of the sky and telling of eternal love. Ransack earth for metaphors, and they fall short of the truth. Words fail to express his beauty, his loveliness: let us try to reflect his glory." (Meyer)

iii. Some things are beautiful from one angle, and not from another. Some are beautiful when they are younger, but not when they are older. Some things look beautiful from a distance, but not up close. Some things are beautiful in one way, but not in another. Jesus is **altogether lovely**; yet for all of His beauty and perfection, it is almost entirely unappreciated by the world. "The vain world cannot see in him a virtue to admire. It is a blind world, a fool world, a world that lieth in the wicked one. Not to discern the beauties of Jesus is an evidence of terrible depravity. Have you, my dear friend, frankly to confess that you were never enamoured of him who was holy, harmless, and undefiled, and went about doing good?" (Spurgeon)

f. **This is my beloved, and this is my friend, O daughters of Jerusalem**: The maiden assured herself of how highly she prized her **beloved**, happily calling him her **friend**. We sense a confidence and strength of conviction in these words.

i. "The Bride replies by describing him in all the wealth of oriental imagery. Yet any other woman might have used every figure in describing her beloved. But, at last, and as I think half unconsciously, the truth is out as she said: 'This is *my* beloved, and this is *my* friend.'" (Morgan)

ii. **This is my friend**: "A common Old Testament word, *rea* expresses companionship and friendship without the overtones of sexual partnership...friendship goes far deeper than mere sexual compatibility and excitement. Happy is the husband or wife whose spouse is also a friend." (Carr)

iii. "The Song of Solomon is unabashedly erotic. Yet it is never satisfied to be content with the physical alone. A normal person finds the erotic ultimately meaningful only if there is trust and commitment, delight in the other's person as well as in their body. The writer of the Song understands this. Our hero is her lover, but he is more: he is her friend." (Kinlaw)

iv. The conclusion of the maiden leads to the logical question: "Then why were you so slow in responding to his call? How could you risk losing such an **altogether lovely** one?" Brought back to a fresh appreciation of the one she loved, the maiden was all the more sorrowful for her prior selfish response.

v. A wife may think that this is the kind of man she could love; but she should probably remember that at one time, her husband *was* this kind of man. She can see him that way again. Instead of thinking "I deserve better than him," she started being amazed at what she once had and still does. Of course, the exact same reasoning applies to a husband in reference to his wife.

Song of Solomon 6 - Reunited in Love

A. The maiden describes a restoration of their love relationship.

1. (1) A further question from the Daughters of Jerusalem.

Where has your beloved gone,
O fairest among women?
Where has your beloved turned aside,
That we may seek him with you?

> a. **Where has your beloved gone, O fairest among women**: Continuing the thought from the previous chapter, it is difficult to tell if these on looking friends are supporting the maiden or being sarcastic towards her.

> b. **Where has your beloved turned aside, that we may seek him with you**: More important than the *tone* of the question in the previous line was this second question. After hearing the impressive description of the character and appearance of the **beloved**, the Daughters of Jerusalem wanted to know where the **beloved** was, and if they could help her locate him.

2. (2-3) The maiden describes her relationship to her beloved man.

My beloved has gone to his garden,
To the beds of spices,
To feed *his flock* in the gardens,
And to gather lilies.
I *am* my beloved's,
And my beloved *is* mine.
He feeds *his flock* among the lilies.

> a. **My beloved has gone to his garden, to the beds of spices**: Previously in the Song of Solomon (Song of Solomon 4:12, 4:16, and 5:1) the image of the **garden** was used to represent the sexuality of the maiden.

> > i. Yet here that image seems out of place; if the **beloved** had **gone to his garden**, then why did it seem that the maiden was still searching

for him? It seems best to regard this as a simple reference to a literal **garden**. The maiden remembered that her **beloved** would be a familiar outdoor place **to feed is flock in the gardens**.

ii. Interestingly, the maiden's previous search through the city accomplished nothing and in fact only harmed her. Yet when she (in response to the questions from the Daughters of Jerusalem) thought about how wonderful her beloved was and where he might be, she was able to figure it out.

iii. "The bride's response to the friends' inquiry assures them that she has not really lost him. The anxiety in her dream was without foundation in reality." (Kinlaw)

iv. Her initial reaction to their relationship problems was entirely feeling-based with little or no thought behind the reaction. When she began to think through the fundamentals of her relationship (Who is my beloved? Where can I find him?), things began to make sense.

v. This reminds us that for success in a Christian marriage, we must *think* and *understand*. The world relies upon mistaken ideas of romantic love and feelings to make marriage work, and never really makes a person *think* and *understand* about marriage.

b. **To feed his flock in the gardens, and to gather lilies**: When the maiden thought about where her beloved would be, she remembered that he would be doing his work (**to feed his flock**) and looking for ways to show his love to her (**to gather lilies**).

i. We can say that the maiden understood some basic things that contributed to the restoration of relationship.

- She knew where he had gone – to his favorite (literal) garden.
- She knew that though they were separated, they still belonged to each other.
- She knew her husband was like a gentle shepherd, who would want to restore the relationship.

c. **I am my beloved's, and my beloved is mine**: The remembrance of these things – who her beloved is, where she is, and what he would be doing – filled the maiden with a renewed sense of their connection and oneness with each other.

i. This is where she wanted to be; this is opposite to the attitude of self-indulgence and laziness shown in the first part of Song of Solomon 5. She is back where she wanted to be, but she did not get there by focusing on her own feelings; rather by thinking and understanding. *Now* feelings came into the picture, and in a wonderful way.

ii. **I am my beloved's, and my beloved is mine** is also an important description of the idea of *oneness*. The maiden sensed and valued their spiritual, emotional, physical, and life connection. From the Apostle Paul's strong and repeated exhortations of this principle of oneness to husbands (and from life experience), one might reasonably understand that women tend to sense and value oneness in marriage by instinct; men have to learn to sense and value it.

iii. "The ability of a couple to succeed in their marriage is equal to the ability of that couple to forgive and accept forgiveness.... When this willingness on the part of both becomes a habit, then the bubble of romance that began their relationship will become a diamond that will last forever." (Glickman)

iv. In Song of Solomon 2:16 the maiden said: *My beloved is mine, and I am his.* Here she says, **I am my beloved's, and my beloved is mine**. Some people note that in the first the emphasis is on *what belongs to her*; in the second the emphasis is on *whom she belongs to*. Perhaps she found it was a more wonderful thing for her to belong to him than for her to "have" him.

B. Enjoyment of the restored relationship.

1. (4-7) The beloved describes the physical appearance of his maiden.

O my love, you *are as* **beautiful as Tirzah,**
Lovely as Jerusalem,
Awesome as *an army* **with banners!**
Turn your eyes away from me,
For they have overcome me.
Your hair *is* **like a flock of goats**
Going down from Gilead.
Your teeth *are* **like a flock of sheep**
Which have come up from the washing;
Every one bears twins,
And none *is* **barren among them.**
Like a piece of pomegranate
Are **your temples behind your veil.**

a. **O my love**: These are the words of the beloved to the maiden. They are together again, and the warmth of their restored relationship is evident in this section.

b. **You are as beautiful as Tizrah, lovely as Jerusalem, awesome as an army with banners**: The beloved compared the beauty and stature of the maiden to noble and beautiful cities (**Tizrah** and **Jerusalem**). She was as impressive as an **army with banners**, ready for battle.

> i. "Tirzah was an ancient Canaanite center that served as the capital of the northern kingdom before Omri (c. 879 B.C.) established Samaria as the capital. This reference is a strong indication of an early date for the origin of the Song." (Kinlaw)

> ii. "Tirzah was a city in the tribe of Ephraim, (Joshua 12:24,) and the capital of that district. It appears to have been *beautiful* in *itself*, and *beautifully situated*, for *Jeroboam* made it his residence before *Samaria* was built; and it seems to have been the ordinary residence of the kings of *Israel*, 1 Kings 14:17; 15:21; 16:6. Its *name* signifies *beautiful* or *delightful*." (Clarke)

> iii. There is not a hint of bitterness or unforgiveness on the part of the beloved. There had been a disruption of their relationship (shown in Song of Solomon 5:2-8) that was largely her fault. Yet the offended party in this relationship was quick to forgive and restore relationship.

c. **Turn your eyes away from me, for they have overcome me**: This was high praise, expressed with poetic beauty. "Look away – I am so excited by the beauty of your eyes that I can't take it!"

> i. "Her eyes have been noted as very beautiful and seductive several times already (Song of Solomon 1:15; 4:1, 9), and the motif is carried out here." (Carr)

> ii. "But it is otherwise in Christ: majesty and love, even unto ravishment, meet in his holy heart. If the Church be sick of love toward him, she should know that he is overcome with love towards her, and that there is no love lost betwixt them." (Trapp)

> iii. Spurgeon related Song of Solomon 6:5 to Jesus and the church, noting that Jesus is overcome with love when He looks upon the church. This was true before the incarnation, as He walked this earth, and now that He has ascended into heaven.

> > • The eyes that show repentance overcome Him.

> > • The eyes that mourn over sin overcome Him.

> > • The eyes that look to Jesus for salvation overcome Him.

> > • The eyes that long for assurance of salvation overcome Him.

> > • The eyes that trust Him and look to Him for all provision overcome Him.

- They eyes of prayer overcome Him.

d. **Your hair is like a flock of goats...**: The beloved continued to describe the maiden, using many of the same images previously used in Song of Solomon 4:1-5. When she returned to him, he told her the same kind of things he told her on their wedding night. It was his way of saying, "I love you and value you just as much now as then."

i. Yet, he avoided description of her more sensual physical features – lips, breasts (as he had described), or hips (as he will later describe). He wanted to avoid the idea that the only reason he wanted to make up with her was to make her willing for sex. This was both good and wise of the beloved.

ii. At the same time in the following verses he *added* some compliments that were good for the sake of reconciliation, reminding her how favorably she compared to others.

2. (8-10) The beloved describes his maiden as compared to other women.

There are sixty queens
And eighty concubines,
And virgins without number.
My dove, my perfect one,
Is the only one,
The only one of her mother,
The favorite of the one who bore her.
The daughters saw her
And called her blessed,
The queens and the concubines,
And they praised her.
Who is she who looks forth as the morning,
Fair as the moon,
Clear as the sun,
Awesome as *an army* with banners?

a. **There are sixty queens and eighty concubines, and virgins without number. My dove, my perfect one, is the only one**: This goes beyond the description of the maiden's beauty recorded in the previous verse. Here he praises the maiden *in comparison to* other women. It is important – even vital – for a wife to feel not only beautiful but *preferred above others* in the eyes of her husband.

i. "He did not go off in a dream world, feel sorry for himself, and wish he had married someone else. Such an attitude, in fact, would only have compounded the problem. Quite the opposite, he very creatively and compassionately assured her of his forgiveness. She was still the girl he married, and he was thankful for her." (Glickman)

b. **Queens...concubines...virgins**: The mention of these other women makes us wonder if Solomon wrote this when he had more than one wife (he eventually had 700 wives and 300 concubines according to 1 Kings 11:3).

> i. The beauty and intensity of the romantic love described in the Song of Solomon does not seem to come from a man who actually romanced and loved many woman (and they came to ruin him spiritually according to 1 Kings 11:1-4). There are a few possible explanations for this problem:
>
> - Solomon wrote this as a young man on the occasion of his *first* love, his *true* love. Of all the 700 wives, *one* had to be first, and the maiden of the Song of Solomon was this one. If this is true, then the reference to the **queens**, **concubines**, and **virgins** was simply theoretical and does not describe women that actually belonged Solomon.
>
> - Solomon wrote this as a middle-aged man with many wives and concubines (though perhaps somewhat early in the count), meaning that he wrote this about an ideal that he did not live or benefit from. If this is true, then the reference to the **queens**, **concubines**, and **virgins** is literal.
>
> - Solomon wrote this as a man late in life, having tasted the good and ideal but wasting the vast majority of his life upon foolish romances and sexual liaisons; he wrote this remembering the ideal and attempting to promote it to others. If this is true, then the reference to the **queens**, **concubines**, and **virgins** is theoretical.
>
> ii. "The relatively small numbers, *sixty* and *eighty*, are supposed by Delitzsch to indicate this episode took place early in Solomon's reign before his harem grew to its fullest number. More probably, no particular harem is being considered. Note the text does not say 'Solomon has' or 'I have', but it is a simple declaration: *There are...*and my beloved *is unique*." (Carr)

c. **The only one of her mother, the favorite of the one who bore her**: This statement is difficult to understand; **the only one** should probably be understood as not meaning that she had no siblings (brothers and sisters seem to be indicated in Song of Solomon 8:8). Instead it emphasizes her preferred and **favorite** status.

d. **The daughters saw her and called her blessed, the queens and concubines, and they praised her**: The greatness and beauty of the maiden was evident not only to the beloved, but also to her woman companions (and theoretical rivals).

i. "One of the best ways to praise someone is to mention the nice things other people have said about that person." (Glickman)

e. **Fair as the moon, clear as the sun, awesome as an army with banners**: This high and poetic praise assured the maiden that her relationship with her beloved was truly reconciled. There was no lingering bitterness or withheld forgiveness.

i. He "did not fall prey to the destructiveness of wounded pride. He did not act in petty revenge; he did not determine to 'get back' at his wife. He thought only of assuring her of his forgiveness." (Glickman)

ii. "Solomon showed us a better way. He did not make Shulamith pay for her insensitivity. He worked on the problem, not on the person. He wanted reconciliation, not retaliation." (Estes)

iii. Spurgeon considered how the church was also **awesome as an army with banners**, emphasizing the idea of the banner and how the church should be like an army bearing **banners**.

- Banners were carried for *distinction*, so that the army could be clearly identified.

- Banners were carried for *discipline*, so that the army could be organized in its work.

- Banners were carried as a sign of *activity*, indicating that something was about to happen.

- Banners were carried as a sign of *confidence*, willing to engage the enemy.

3. (11-12) The maiden describes her meeting with the beloved.

I went down to the garden of nuts
To see the verdure of the valley,
To see whether the vine had budded
***And* the pomegranates had bloomed.**
Before I was even aware,
My soul had made me
***As* the chariots of my noble people.**

a. **I went down to the garden**: Presumably, this is where the beloved was (Song of Solomon 6:2). She happily remembered their reuniting.

i. Watchman Nee gives an example of over-spiritualization here: "Nuts – with their hard shells which require careful cracking before the delicious and nourishing interiors can be extracted – may be likened to the Word of God, which yields its soul-satisfying meats only to those who diligently and with prayer seek to rightly divide the word of truth."

b. **To see the verdure of the valley, to see whether the vine had budded**: She went to see and to enjoy the coming of *spring*. Springtime was associated (perhaps both literally and symbolically) with the presence and goodness of their love (Song of Solomon 2:10-13). Their relationship was in springtime again.

i. "Guilt had turned her eyes inward, but he brought them outward. She went down to the garden in self-conscious guilt in hope of renewal, and she was met with praise which turned her eyes from herself to him, and once to him, back to herself through eyes of forgiveness." (Glickman)

c. **Before I was even aware, my soul had made me as the chariots of my noble people**: The reuniting of their relationship, the return of springtime for their love, was so exhilarating to her that the maiden felt that her **soul** was as a free and as fast as a **chariot**.

i. The goodness and depth of their relationship really had been restored. Problems of the past didn't mean that their future was doomed or even hindered. Couples should be confident in faith, knowing that God can restore and bring springtime to troubled relationships.

ii. The following verse implies that perhaps the maiden was actually in a moving chariot; perhaps the prestigious chariot of her beloved, Solomon. The double-meaning of this would strengthen the idea of a complete restoration of relationship, as he honored his maiden with this prestigious luxury. The Revised Standard Version translates with this idea: *Before I was aware, my fancy set me in a chariot beside my prince.*

4. (13a) The Daughters of Jerusalem appeal to the maiden.

Return, return, O Shulamite;
Return, return, that we may look upon you!

a. **Return, return, O Shulamite**: The words seem to have spoken by the Daughters of Jerusalem (or perhaps by the beloved and his friends). They appealed to the maiden who seems to be swept away as in a chariot (Song of Solomon 6:12), perhaps both literally and figuratively.

i. This is the only verse in the Song of Solomon where the name **Shulamite** is used. It may indicate someone from the Galilean village of Shunam; or the name may also simply be the feminine form of the name *Solomon*, indicating their close unity.

ii. "In the original language in which this song was written, 'Shulamith' was simply the feminine form of the name Solomon, the name of the king. It would be like 'Don and Donna' in our language. The name would thus mean that she was the feminine counterpart of Solomon, his opposite number." (Glickman)

b. **Return, return, that we may look upon you**: The idea is of the speakers calling out to a departing chariot. They wanted the maiden to return so that they might continue enjoying her beauty and goodness, now made more beautiful because of the lovingly restored relationship she enjoyed.

5. (13b) The response of the maiden to the Daughters of Jerusalem.

What would you see in the Shulamite—
As it were, the dance of the two camps?

a. **What would you see in the Shulamite**: The response of the maiden to the plea of the Daughters of Jerusalem shows she has a fundamental humility. She seemed surprised at the attention she received.

i. Some believe that this half-verse is from the beloved, speaking to the Daughters of Jerusalem, and this is possible. "The king remarks in fact that they loved to gaze upon her as intensely as if they were looking upon a festive dance." (Glickman)

b. **As it were, the dance of the two camps**: This statement is difficult to understand. Perhaps it refers to a literal **dance**, as if the maiden was dancing and calling out to the on looking Daughters of Jerusalem. Others emphasize the idea of **two camps** and think it refers to the internal battle of the soul and is a mention of the inner battles the maiden has fought and is fighting.

i. "Suggestions of some sort of sword dance or celebration of bloody military victory seem out of place here." (Carr)

ii. "In v.13 the bride responds to the guests who want to see her. She is modestly reluctant. She questions their desire. If she wonders why anyone would want to see her, she is to get an answer from her lover. The next unit is his description of her charms." (Kinlaw)

Song of Solomon 7 - The Maiden's Beauty

A. The maiden is described for a third time.

1. (1-3) Description of the maiden's body.

How beautiful are your feet in sandals,
O prince's daughter!
The curves of your thighs *are* **like jewels,**
The work of the hands of a skillful workman.
Your navel *is* **a rounded goblet;**
It lacks no blended beverage.
Your waist *is* **a heap of wheat**
Set about with lilies.
Your two breasts *are* **like two fawns,**
Twins of a gazelle.

> a. **How beautiful are your feet in sandals, O prince's daughter**: This begins another extended description of the maiden's beauty. Song of Solomon 6:13 ended with both a request for the maiden to return so her beauty could be longer enjoyed, and a gentle protest from the maiden wondering why she should be such a subject of attention.
>
> > i. The mention of *the dance of the two camps* in Song of Solomon 6:13 suggests that the maiden was dancing. This is also suggested by the description of these verses, which begins at her feet and continues up her body to her head. This would be much more natural in describing someone who was standing and dancing. Yet did she dance before a group of onlookers or privately for her beloved?
> >
> > ii. There are some reasons to believe that this was a dance before a group of onlookers, such as or including the Daughters of Jerusalem.
> >
> > - The inherited context from Song of Solomon 6:13, with a call from the Daughters of Jerusalem.

- The description of the maiden as the **prince's daughter** seems more appropriate from those other than the beloved.

- The description of *a king* in Song of Solomon 7:5 may be more appropriate in the voice of someone other than the beloved.

iii. There are also some reasons to believe that this was a private dance for the beloved; mainly, the description suggests that the maiden's **thighs**, **navel**, **waist**, and **breasts** could all be seen (at least partially). There is nothing in Biblical or ancient Hebrew culture or in the Song of Solomon itself to suggest that it was a practice for a maiden to dance provocatively before a public group. Given this, it is probable that this is merely a poetic image and not a news report, *or* a private display for the blessing and benefit of the beloved.

iv. It is also important to notice that this is the *third* extended description of the maiden's beauty (previously also in Song of Solomon 4:1-5 and 6:4-9). These three descriptions may be compared to the single description of the beloved's appearance (found in Song of Solomon 5:10-16), which was not even spoken to the beloved himself, but to others about the beloved. This comparison strengthens the impression that it is far more important for a woman to be assured of and confident in her beauty than it is for a man.

- The first description of beauty (Song of Solomon 4:1-5) is in the context of the wedding night; the beloved praised the beauty of the maiden before she yielded her virginity to him.

- The second description of beauty (Song of Solomon 6:4-9) is the context of restoring a relationship after a conflict; the beloved assured the maiden that she was just as beautiful to him then as she was on the wedding night.

- This third description of beauty (Song of Solomon 7:1-5) is perhaps a more public description, further assuring the maiden of her beauty.

v. "It should be noticed that, though the Song is really the bride's song there are three occasions when the groom describes her beauty in detail and only one where she reciprocates. If the Song has any allegorical significance, it should indicate that God finds us much more delightful than we find him." (Kinlaw)

vi. **Prince's daughter**: "As in 6:12, the meaning is not necessarily that the girl is of royal birth, but rather that she is of gracious and noble character and person." (Carr)

b. **How beautiful are your feet in sandals**: As the maiden danced, the onlookers naturally first noticed her **feet in sandals**. They admired both the beauty of her **feet** and her **sandals**.

c. **The curves of your thighs...your navel...your waist**: The description visually moves up from the feet of the maiden, describing the beauty of her body.

> i. If we assume that these are the comments of the beloved made in a private setting, the comment of Glickman makes sense: "One of the things we notice is that the praise of the king is much more sensual and intimate. It reflects a greater knowledge of they physical beauty of his wife. For example, here he praises the curves of her thigh and soft warmth of her stomach." (Glickman)

> ii. "Wine and wheat were the basic foods of any meal. His joining these two images in his praise of her stomach must mean that her stomach is like a wonderful feast to him." (Glickman)

> iii. "The reference to the lilies that encircle the stomach reminds us that we are dealing with figures whose very ambiguity enrich the eroticism of the passage." (Kinlaw)

> iv. The comments of the old Puritan commentator John Trapp show the difficulty of approaching the text primarily as a spiritual allegory. "The navel is baptism, that nourisheth newborn babes in the womb of the Church.... Some understand hereby that other sacrament of the Lord's Supper, called a 'heap of wheat,' for its store of excellent nourishment." (Trapp)

> v. **Set about with lilies**: Some believe that this is a poetic reference to the pubic region, describing the maiden's naked body. This is unlikely, especially given the use of **lilies** in Song of Solomon 4:5 and 5:13.

d. **Your two breasts are like two fawns**: This is an image repeated from the first description of the maiden in Song of Solomon 4:1-5. There as well as here the emphasis seems to be on the idea is that the maiden's breasts look as innocent and attractive as young deer, as well as matching in their form and beauty (**twins of a gazelle**).

> i. Trapp can't escape the instinct to make these **two breasts** something other than two female breasts. "Fresh and lusty, even and equal. Understand the two Testaments; hereunto resembled for their perfect agreement, amiable proportion, and swift running all the world over in a short time." (Trapp)

> ii. "This poem indicates the perpetual charm of the female form to the male." (Kinlaw)

2. (4-5) Description of the maiden's head, face, and hair.

Your neck *is* like an ivory tower,
Your eyes *like* the pools in Heshbon
By the gate of Bath Rabbim.
Your nose *is* like the tower of Lebanon
Which looks toward Damascus.
Your head *crowns* you like *Mount* Carmel,
And the hair of your head *is* like purple;
A king *is* held captive by *your* tresses.

a. **Your neck is like an ivory tower**: The idea with this image isn't so much of an extremely long neck, but of one that communicate nobility and strength of character.

i. "He is probably complimenting not only the noble dignity exemplified in her posture but also the artistic smoothness of her neck. As he gently slid his fingers down her neck it was smooth as ivory to him." (Glickman)

b. **Your eyes like the pools in Heshbon**: Here the deep beauty of the maiden's eyes is described. Perhaps there was something particularly beautiful about these specific **pools** of water.

i. "Possibly here were two fish-pools, which being conveniently seated in a large field, might bear some resemblance to the eyes placed in the head." (Poole)

c. **Your nose is like the tower of Lebanon which looks toward Damascus**: It seems that the **tower of Lebanon** was not a literal tower, but a hill or mountain whose white cliffs looked out **toward Damascus**. This would make this a reference more to the color of the maiden's nose than the size or shape of it.

i. "*Lebanon* is one of several words derived from the Hebrew root *laben*, 'to be white'. It was probably the whiteness of the limestone cliffs that gave the mountain its name. This suggests that the imagery here is associated with the colour of her nose rather than its shape or size. Her face is pale, like the ivory tone of her neck, not sunburnt." (Carr)

d. **Your head crowns you...a king is held captive by your tresses**: The beauty of her hair is so striking that it can only be related to *royalty* (**is like purple**) and captivates royals (**a king is held captive**).

i. **Tresses**: "The root meaning is to run or flow, so that the picture here is of her hair having the appearance of running, rippling water." (Carr)

ii. "On their wedding night he could give sevenfold praise, but on this later night he could give tenfold praise. Their love had truly deepened." (Glickman)

3. (6-9a) Description of the beloved's desire.

How fair and how pleasant you are,
O love, with your delights!
This stature of yours is like a palm tree,
And your breasts *like* its clusters.
I said, "I will go up to the palm tree,
I will take hold of its branches."
Let now your breasts be like clusters of the vine,
The fragrance of your breath like apples,
And the roof of your mouth like the best wine.

a. **How fair and how pleasant you are, O love**: Here it seems clear that it is the beloved speaking, and not a group such as the Daughters of Jerusalem. If it is true that such a group spoke the words of Song of Solomon 7:1-5, then clearly now the beloved speaks to his maiden more directly about his attraction to her and desire for her.

i. **With your delights** indicates how basic and wonderful his attraction was to her. She delighted him; obviously with her beauty and personality, but also with her character and strength.

ii. By analogy and application, the great delight of the beloved over his maiden helps us to understand that this shows us how much God loves us. *As the bridegroom rejoices over the bride, so shall your God rejoice over you.* (Isaiah 62:5)

iii. "Dear soul, do you realize the desire of your Beloved towards you? You love Him; but He loves you ever so much more. You desire Him; but his desire towards you is as much greater than yours towards Him, as sunlight is more brilliant than moonlight." (Meyer)

b. **This stature of yours is like a palm tree**: Here he speaks of the maiden as being tall and noble like a great **palm tree**. It is another reference to more than her beauty, but her character and bearing as well.

c. **And your breasts like its clusters.... Let now your breasts be like clusters of the vine**: Seeing the great character and beauty of his maiden, the beloved *wanted her*. He loved her for more than her body, but he also – rightfully – wanted to enjoy the pleasures of her **breasts** and body in married lovemaking.

i. Solomon had advice with the same spirit in Proverbs: *Let your fountain be blessed, and rejoice with the wife of your youth. As a loving deer and a graceful doe, let her breasts satisfy you at all times; and always be enraptured with her love. For why should you, my son, be enraptured by an immoral woman, and be embraced in the arms of a seductress?* (Proverbs 5:19-20)

ii. The sense we have from all this is that this couple has grown and matured in their sharing of love, sexual and otherwise. "This is a different mood from the delicate formality of their wedding night." (Glickman)

d. **The fragrance of your breath like apples, and the roof of your mouth like the best wine**: The beloved told his maiden how pleasing and satisfying their lovemaking was to him.

i. "He creates a vivid picture of his kissing her breasts as one would place the clusters of the vine to one's lips. And her kisses would bring the fragrance of her breath like the sweet scent of apples, and her mouth would be 'like the best wine' to be slowly and exquisitely enjoyed with every sip." (Glickman)

B. The maiden longs for intimacy with her beloved.

1. (9b-10) The longing for intimacy.

The wine **goes** *down* **smoothly for my beloved,**
Moving gently the lips of sleepers.
I *am* **my beloved's,**
And his desire *is* **toward me.**

a. **The wine goes down smoothly for my beloved**: This is the maiden's response to the beloved's previous statement and appeal. He said how much he enjoyed their lovemaking; now she answers with recognition of its goodness.

b. **Moving gently the lips of the sleepers**: The idea is of them asleep together, perhaps embracing one another and refreshed in love.

i. "Whereas the wedding night focused on the purpose of sex as the consummation of marriage, this night focuses on the purpose of sex as the nourishment of marriage.... As they fell asleep the last kiss lingered in each other's minds like the aftertaste of good wine. What an enchanting picture of the sleeping couple!" (Glickman)

c. **I am my beloved's and his desire is toward me**: The maiden is completely secure in his love. She understands **his desire** as not a demand or a burden, but as wonderful and appropriate.

i. "She not only places his possession of her primary, but strengthens it by adding that his desire is toward her, and so focused is she upon him that she omits her possession of him. She has really lost herself in him and thereby found herself." (Glickman)

ii. "It is the full, final, ultimate word of love. It expresses complete satisfaction, absolute rest, and uttermost of contentment and peace. There are two elements in it. The first is that of complete abandonment; 'I am my beloved's.' The second is that of the realization that the beloved is satisfied; 'His desire is toward me.'" (Morgan)

2. (11-13) The invitation to intimacy.

Come, my beloved,
Let us go forth to the field;
Let us lodge in the villages.
Let us get up early to the vineyards;
Let us see if the vine has budded,
***Whether* the grape blossoms are open,**
***And* the pomegranates are in bloom.**
There I will give you my love.
The mandrakes give off a fragrance,
And at our gates *are* pleasant *fruits*,
All manner, new and old,
Which I have laid up for you, my beloved.

a. **Come, my beloved, let us go forth to the field; let us lodge in the villages**: Responding to the desire of her beloved, the maiden invited him to come away on a trip to the countryside where they could enjoy their intimacy. It was like a weekend get-away for a couple deeply in love.

i. Earlier the beloved made a similar invitation to the maiden: *Rise up, my love, my fair one, and come away* (Song of Solomon 2:10). Now the maiden answered with a similar invitation. She seems to have matured in her self-confidence since the early days of their courtship (Song of Solomon 1:5-6). She also understood that it was not only the responsibility of the man to signal the desire for intimacy.

ii. "If we must at any time listen to the praises of our virtues, if we have served God so that the Church recognises and rewards our usefulness, it is well for us to listen just as long as we are obliged to do, but no longer; and then let us turn aside at once to something more practical and more healthful to our own spirits. The spouse seems abruptly to break off from listening to the song of the virgins, and turns to her own husband- Lord, communion with whom is ever blessed and ever profitable, and she says to him, 'Come, my beloved, let us go forth into the field.'" (Spurgeon)

b. **Let us get up early to the vineyards; let us see if the vine has budded**: Since springtime was a special emblem of their love (Song of Solomon 2:10-13 and 6:11-12). She used that image to communicate her own desire to enjoy the freshness and strength of their love and intimacy.

 i. "The poet thus reveals that their relationship has gone from spring to spring, that now it has experienced a full cycle of growth." (Glickman)

c. **There I will give you my love**: The maiden was refreshingly honest and open with her beloved. She said to him, "Let's get away to the countryside and make love." This is an invitation likely to appeal to a husband.

 i. In all of this we see a remarkable freedom and joy in their love. Sexual intimacy was not understood to be the husband's pleasure and the wife's duty; there is a spirit throughout the Song of Solomon that shows how good marital love can be for both partners.

 ii. "Song of Solomon teaches that true freedom does not come by someone's being liberated *from* marriage. The truth is that genuine liberation comes *in* marriage. Marriage is a secure hedge that protects love as it grows. As love is nurtured, it produces freedom and fulfillment." (Estes)

d. **The mandrakes give off a fragrance**: This plant was understood to be an aphrodisiac in the ancient world, especially in the sense of increasing fertility (Genesis 30:14-17).

 i. "The *mandrake* or 'love apple' is a pungently fragrant plant that has long been considered an aphrodisiac – not that these lovers needed any additional stimulation, but the use of such items has long been part of the lore of love-making." (Carr)

 ii. Therefore the reference to **mandrakes** shows a desire for children. "Shulamith wanted children as a visible demonstration of the oneness in her and Solomon's love." (Estes)

e. **All manner, new and old, which I have laid up for you, my beloved**: This difficult to translate phrase may have the sense that she is inviting him to enjoy intimacy in ways that are both familiar and new to the couple. The idea would be they would enjoy their lovemaking in creative ways that were planned in advance by the maiden (**which I have laid up for you**).

Song of Solomon 8 - On Mountains of Spices

A. The maiden's loving words.

1. (1-2) The maiden's passion for her beloved.

Oh, that you were like my brother,
Who nursed at my mother's breasts!
***If* I should find you outside,**
I would kiss you;
I would not be despised.
I would lead you *and* bring you
Into the house of my mother,
She *who* used to instruct me.
I would cause you to drink of spiced wine,
Of the juice of my pomegranate.

> a. **Oh, that you were like my brother.... If I should find you outside, I would kiss you**: The maiden's idea is based on the cultural acceptance of some public displays of affection between brother and sister. She wished that she could be as open with her beloved as she would be allowed to be with her actual **brother**.

> > i. "She would like the liberty in public that the brother and sister in that day had. So she wishes she could freely kiss him in public." (Kinlaw)

> b. **I would lead you and bring you into the house of my mother**: The maiden wanted to enjoy the intimacy of married love with her beloved, but to enjoy in the context of the approval of their family. There was nothing impure or secretive about their love.

> > i. **Lead**: "The verb is used nearly ninety times in the Old Testament, with the meaning 'teach' or 'learn'...the teacher is the mother who has instructed her daughter in the 'facts of life' and it is to that 'schoolroom'

she wants to return to show how well she has learned her lessons." (Carr)

ii. "In this moment of deepest intimacy, when no prying eyes are wanted, she thinks of her mother and her friends.... Again we are reminded that we are social creatures inextricably bound up in a web of human relations." (Kinlaw)

iii. **Spiced wine**: "Wine rendered peculiarly strong and invigorating. The bride and bridegroom on the wedding day both drank out of the same cup, to show that they were to *enjoy* and equally *bear* together the *comforts* and *adversities* of life." (Clarke)

2. (3-4) The maiden's plea to the Daughters of Jerusalem.

His left hand *is* under my head,
And his right hand embraces me.
I charge you, O daughters of Jerusalem,
Do not stir up nor awaken love
Until it pleases.

a. **His left hand is under my head**: This phrase was used before in Song of Solomon 2:6, describing the maiden's desire for lovemaking. The idea is that the maiden is reclined and her beloved caresses her with **his right hand** (perhaps intimately).

b. **I charge you, O daughters of Jerusalem, do not stir up nor awaken love until it pleases**: This is the third time that this phrase is used in the Song of Solomon (previously at 2:7 and 3:5). As before, this idea can be understood as a plea to leave her sweet romantic dream uninterrupted. Or, it can be understood both in the context of *relationship* and in *passion*.

i. In terms of relationship it means, "Let our love progress and grow until it is matured and fruitful, making a genuinely pleasing relationship – *don't let us go too fast.*" In terms of passion it means, "Let our love making continue without interruption until we are both fulfilled. Don't let us start until we can go all the way."

ii. "What is this warning? That love is so sacred a thing that it must not be trifled with. It is not to be sought. It stirs and awakens of itself. To trifle with the capacity for it, is to destroy that very capacity." (Morgan)

iii. "The reader having just seen their lovely portrait of marriage might be tempted more than ever to force such a relationship in impatience." (Glickman)

B. Final words from the loving couple, their family, and their friends.

1. (5) A relative speaks to the loving couple.

Who *is* this coming up from the wilderness,
Leaning upon her beloved?
I awakened you under the apple tree.
There your mother brought you forth;
There she *who* bore you brought *you* forth.

a. **Who is this coming up from the wilderness, leaning upon her beloved**: As with a few passages in the Song of Solomon, it is difficult to say with certainty who the speaker and the intended hearer are with these words. Perhaps it is best to simply assign it to an observer, either a relative (such as the maiden's brothers who will be mentioned later) or one of the Daughters of Jerusalem.

b. **Leaning upon her beloved**: The idea here is not that the maiden is old and infirmed; rather that she simply accompanies her beloved and walks with him in the closeness characteristic of husband and wife.

i. Charles Spurgeon used this as a picture of the closeness and dependence of the Church upon Jesus Christ. Many things could be said as true regarding both the maiden and the people of God.

- She leaned because she was weak and needed strength.

- She leaned because the way was long.

- She leaned because the way was perilous.

- She leaned because the path was ascending, going higher and higher.

- She leaned because her progress took her more and more away from others and more and more to her beloved's side.

- She leaned because she was sure her beloved was strong enough to bear her weight.

- She leaned because she loved him.

ii. "Beloved, there is no part of the pilgrimage of a saint in which he can afford to walk in any other way but in the way of leaning. He cometh up at the first, and he cometh up at the last, still leaning, still leaning upon Christ Jesus; ay, and leaning more and more heavily upon Christ the older he grows." (Spurgeon)

c. **I awakened you under the apple tree**: The speaker reminds the couple of their youth and family roots. They were now grown and happily married but still connected to and the product of their families.

i. "Or it may be understood of the following circumstance: The bridegroom found her once asleep under an apple tree, and awoke

Song of Solomon 8 177

her; and this happened to be the very place where her mother, taken in untimely labour, had brought her into the world." And here the bridegroom, in his fondness and familiarity, recalls these little adventures to her memory." (Clarke)

2. (6-7) The maiden describes the strength of her love.

Set me as a seal upon your heart,
As a seal upon your arm;
For love *is as* strong as death,
Jealousy *as* cruel as the grave;
Its flames *are* flames of fire,
A most vehement flame.
Many waters cannot quench love,
Nor can the floods drown it.
If a man would give for love
All the wealth of his house,
It would be utterly despised.

a. **Set me as a seal upon your heart, as a seal upon your arm**: Using this strong image of a **seal**, the maiden appeals to her beloved, asking him to recognize the permanence of their commitment.

i. Married love should be like a **seal**, in the sense that a seal speaks of permanence, belonging, and security. "Her love is so total and so strong that she wants their mutual possession of each other to be as lasting as life. It is a strongly poetic demand for 'until death do us part.'" (Kinlaw)

b. **For love is as strong as death**: The maiden considered that love was like **death** in its permanence and strength. Death is **strong** enough to make every man answer to it; love is much the same way and the strength of romantic love is more powerful than many powerful men (Samson as one example).

c. **Jealousy as cruel as the grave**: It is hard to know if this was meant in a positive or a negative sense. There is a **jealousy** that is good and appropriate in the marriage relationship, and there is another aspect of **jealousy** that is corrosive and destructive. In the context, it is more likely that this speaks of the unrelenting desire for appropriate oneness that is not broken by a romantic competitor.

i. We should have a jealously in our heart regarding our love for Jesus, hating anything that might come between Him and us. He certainly has such a jealousy towards us.

ii. "Whenever love absorbs the heart, jealousy will guard the object of affection. Only let a provocation occur, something of jealousy is sure to appear. Your love to Christ especially lacks the genuine stamp if it is never roused to jealousy by the malice of foes and the faithlessness of professed friends of our Lord. Many Christians nowadays have a kind of love which is too fond of ease, and too full of compromise to kindle any jealousy in their breasts." (Spurgeon)

d. **Its flames are the flames of fire, a most vehement flame**: The idea is that love is like a fire, with great power and usefulness – for good or even for destruction. Love has lifted some to great heights; it has consumed others and left only ashes.

i. **A most vehement flame**: The Jerusalem Bible and the American Standard Version take the last syllable of the Hebrew word translated **vehement flame** (*salhebetya*) as being the divine name Yahweh, the LORD. Therefore, they translate, *a flame of Yahweh himself* (JB) and *a very flame of Jehovah* (ASV). "The meaning could be 'love is a flame which has its origin in God'; while this is technically true, the fact that this is the only place in the Song a possible use of the divine name appears militates against this understanding of the final syllable. More likely, this is simply a use of a standard idiom for the superlative." (Carr)

ii. "More forcible is the language of the original — 'The coals thereof are the coals of God,' — a Hebrew idiom to express the most glowing of all flames — 'the coals of God!' as though it were no earthly flame, but something far superior to the most vehement affection among men." (Spurgeon)

iii. "The love on which a beautiful love is built is a persevering flame burning as brightly at the beginning as it does later on." (Glickman)

e. **If a man would give for love all the wealth of his house, it would be utterly despised**: This phrase reflects the sentiment of a popular song from many years ago, that "money can't buy me love." Love has its own economy, often dramatically separate from our normal financial reckonings.

i. If a man did **give for love all the wealth of his house**, "He would be despised for reducing love and the person from which it comes to an object. If you set the price of love at a billion dollars, you would then reduced it to nothing. By its very nature love must be given. Sex can be bought; love must be given." (Glickman)

ii. All in all, these verses give us four remarkable pictures of love:

- Love is like a seal on the heart and arm. *Therefore*, love belongs to those who are willing to give up something of themselves to another person who is also willing to give up something of themselves.

- Love is like death, in that it is persistent and keeps reaching out; it is total and irreversible. *Therefore*, the bond of love needs to be nourished and regarded as permanent.

- Love is like a raging fire and cannot be extinguished. *Therefore*, one must take care how, where, and with whom the spark of love is ignited.

- Love cannot be bought or sold; it is not a piece of merchandise. *Therefore*, love must be appreciated for its great value and not be taken for granted.

3. (8-9) The maiden's brothers.

We have a little sister,
And she has no breasts.
What shall we do for our sister
In the day when she is spoken for?
If she *is* a wall,
We will build upon her
A battlement of silver;
And if she *is* a door,
We will enclose her
With boards of cedar.

a. **We have a little sister, and she has no breasts**: The idea is that Song of Solomon 8:8-9 is a look back at a planning session held by the maiden's brothers when she was still a fairly young girl. They recognized that they had a responsibility towards her; to plan ahead for the day she would be spoken for – the day of her marriage.

i. Upon this verse, the Puritan John Trapp made a curious comment by allegory: "A society of men without the preaching of the Word is like a mother of children without breasts."

ii. Matthew Poole had another allegorical idea: "This signifies the present doleful state of the Gentiles, which as yet were not grown up into a church estate, and wanted the milk or food of life, as for itself, so also for its members."

b. **What shall we do for our sister in the day when she is spoken for**: The idea is that the brothers wondered what they could do to prepare and protect their sister before her eventual marriage (**when she is spoken for**).

i. We might normally think that this supervisory role would be more assumed by a father in the family instead of brothers. There is no certain explanation as for why the father is not mentioned in this context; there could be any number of reasons.

ii. "Shulamith's brothers took their responsibility seriously, for long before she was of marriageable age they determined to keep her pure for her husband (Song of Solomon 8:9). They resolved to provide guidance and positive pressure to help Shulamith remain a virgin." (Estes)

c. **If she is a wall, we will build upon her...and if she is a door, we will enclose her**: The brothers wisely decided to guide and help their sister according to her own character and choices. If she were like **a wall** that stood effectively against despoilers and exploiters, they would reward, encourage, and **build upon her**. If she were more like **a door** allowing unwise access, they would then restrict her freedoms in her own self-interest (**we will enclose her**).

i. "If she be a wall, built upon the true foundation, strong and stable, she shall be adorned and beautified with battlements of silver; but if unstable and easily moved to and fro like a door, such treatment will be as impossible as unsuitable; she will need to be inclosed with boards of cedar, hedged in with restraints, for her own protection." (Taylor)

ii. "If she could handle responsibility, they would give it to her; if not, she would be restricted." (Glickman)

iii. This presents a principle that is often overlooked in the western world and dangerously over-emphasized in other parts of the world: that the family has a shared responsibility for the purity and romantic supervision of the young of the family.

4. (10) The maiden answers her brothers.

I *am* a wall,
And my breasts like towers;
Then I became in his eyes
As one who found peace.

a. **I am a wall, and my breasts are like towers**: In response to the statement of the brothers the maiden – perhaps leaving the retrospective remembrance and thinking of her present maturity and honorable courtship and marriage – reminds her brothers that in the descriptions they offered (*wall* or *door* in Song of Solomon 8:9), she was and is definitely a strongly defended **wall**, even with the strength of **towers**.

i. The phrase "**my breasts like towers**" does not intend to describe the appearance of her figure, but simply connects with the idea of a *wall* used in this and the previous verse. Her honor was strongly defended.

ii. "She herself had chosen to be a wall. And finally she grew up. Her breasts were like towers. The towers were the fortresses of the land. They inspired a somber appreciation from the citizens and a healthy respect from their enemies." (Glickman)

b. **Then I became in his eyes as one who found peace**: The maiden described her married state. Her blessedness could be described as making her **as one who found peace**. There was a peace, a well-being, a security in her life, flowing in part from the health of her marriage.

i. **Then I became in his eyes as one who found peace**: This slightly changes a familiar Old Testament expression – *to find grace in the eyes of the LORD* (as in Genesis 6:8 in reference to Noah). "Frequently, as in this case, it refers to a girl finding love in the eyes of a man. She is said to have found grace in his eyes. So when this young girl says she has found peace in his eyes, she is saying that she has found romance in Solomon's eyes." (Glickman)

ii. We dare not miss the connection between the wise and noble defense of her honor and virginity described in these and the previous verses, and the health and **peace** she now found in married life. Her **wall**-like character was an important part of the foundation for the blessed married life she now enjoyed.

iii. It was also important that her family encouraged this concern and character development in her from a young age. One reason this is important is that once we experience something – such as premarital sex – the temptation to do it again will be stronger. This is confirmed not only by experience, but also by neurobiology. When we get a chemical/hormonal/biological rush from a physically pleasurably experience, it builds brain circuits that look for a repeat of the same rush. The body also compensates by decreasing the production and contribution of natural and healthy chemical/hormonal/biological agents.

iv. In all this, medical research agrees with the Bible: *His own iniquities entrap the wicked man, and he is caught in the cords of his sin* (Proverbs 5:22). If we fail to be a **wall** against certain sins, we will be *caught in the cords* of those sins, and never know the goodness of becoming **as one who found peace**.

5. (11-12) The maiden understands her value.

Solomon had a vineyard at Baal Hamon;
He leased the vineyard to keepers;
Everyone was to bring for its fruit
A thousand silver coins.
My own vineyard *is* before me.
You, O Solomon, *may have* a thousand,
And those who tend its fruit two hundred.

a. **Solomon had a vineyard...he leased the vineyard to keepers**: The idea in these verses seems to be an appreciation of the cost and value of something. Solomon's **vineyard** had value, and so it cost something to use it.

b. **My own vineyard is before me**: The maiden recognized her own value, and after defending her honor and virginity both in her youth and courtship, she was then able to freely and rightly give it to Solomon (**You, O Solomon, may have a thousand**).

i. "Her own vineyard represents her own person (Song of Solomon 1:6; 2:15). Its 'position' before her emphasizes that she is under her free direction to do with herself as she pleases." (Glickman) And, she chose to give herself to Solomon, her beloved. The entire value of it (**a thousand silver coins**) was given to him.

ii. The attitude of the maiden is quite different from that of most people in modern western culture. She saw genuine *value* in both her virginity and more importantly in *herself*. She was not to be cheaply and easily given away; and therefore, she found a man who truly valued her, estimating her worth correctly and highly.

iii. "Shulamith's life was her vineyard. Because she was pure, she could give herself entirely to her husband. Her heart was undivided, and her body was not tainted by premarital sex." (Estes)

iv. "There is always the possibility, though difficult for us, that the reference to Solomon's vineyard is to be taken literally while the reference to the spouse's vineyard is metaphorical. Jesus did the same kind of thing when he said, 'Destroy this temple, and I will raise it again in three days' (John 2:19)." (Kinlaw)

v. "There are a great many people, who seem to forget that they have a vineyard of their own to keep; or else, if they remember it, they cannot say, 'My vineyard, which is mine, is before me,' for they go about gazing on other people's vineyards, instead of keeping their eyes fixed upon their own. They say, 'Look at So-and-so's vineyard; I don't think he trims his vines in the new style.'" (Spurgeon)

c. **And those who tend its fruit two hundred**: It is a little difficult to understand exactly what the maiden refers to here. In context, it is probably a way of giving credit to her brothers for their concern and effort in guarding her honor before marriage.

> i. "The probability is that references that were easily understandable when written have become problems for us because of distance and its accompanying ignorance of ancient customs." (Kinlaw)

> ii. By analogy, Charles Spurgeon considered that **those who tend its fruit** were pastors and ministers of the gospel, and that they also were due their own **two hundred**. He thought this spoke of the responsibility of a congregation to support their minister.

> iii. "I may, perhaps, have some members of country churches present, who are not kind to their minister. I can speak plainly upon this point, because my people are almost too kind to me; but I say to members of other churches, — Take care of your minister, for you will never get a blessing unless you are kind to him whom God has set over you. If your minister does not have his two hundred, — that is, if he has not your love and respect, and if you do not give him sufficient to keep him above want, — you cannot expect the Spirit of God to work with you. I believe there are scores of churches in which no good is ever done, for this very reason. God says, 'You starve my minister, so I will starve you. You find fault with him, and quarrel with him; then I will find fault with you, and quarrel with you. There shall be no blessing upon you; you shall be like Gilboa, there shall be neither dew nor rain upon you.'" (Spurgeon)

6. (13) The beloved answers his maiden.

You who dwell in the gardens,
The companions listen for your voice—
Let me hear it!

a. **You who dwell in the gardens**: This seems to be the beloved addressing the maiden with this title. She could be called one who did **dwell in the gardens**, in places of delight, well-cared for, and associated with their love (Song of Solomon 4:12-16, 6:2, 6:11).

> i. "In these last two verses we 'overhear' Solomon and Shulamith whispering tenderly to each other." (Estes)

> ii. Because her husband, the beloved, cherished her so much her life was indeed as pleasant as a garden. Dr. Jeff Schloss noted how important it was for a wife to feel this, explaining that husbands and wives rank their happiness in correlation to how much they believe they are loved

and cherished by their spouse. *Wives who do not have the confidence that they are loved and cherished by their husband in fact die sooner, and they die sooner than single women.* These findings are true across cultures.

b. **Let me hear it**: Though others also enjoyed the company of the maiden (**the companions listen for your voice**), the beloved longed to enjoy the blessing of oneness and companionship with his maiden. Therefore, he asked to hear her voice in a place fond to their remembrance.

> i. Some believe that these last two verses speak of a separation between the maiden and her beloved; some business or necessity has kept them apart. She is safe and blessed **in the gardens**, and here the beloved longs to hear her voice. If so, then these closing verses show the relationship strong and blessed, even when the couple cannot be together as much as they would like to be.

> ii. "In other words- when I am far away from thee, fill thou this garden with my name, and let thy heart commune with me." (Spurgeon)

7. (14) The maiden calls out to her beloved.

Make haste, my beloved,
And be like a gazelle
Or a young stag
On the mountains of spices.

a. **Make haste, my beloved**: If we take the suggestion that these last verses speak of a necessary separation between the maiden and the beloved, then this is her response to his desire to hear her voice once again (Song of Solomon 8:13). She calls for him to **make haste**, so they can be reunited.

> i. Thus we see that the Song of Solomon closes with the same sense of passion and intensity with which it opened. It reminds us that though the relationship between the maiden and the beloved aged and matured, it had not lost its passion and excitement.

> ii. "In every way we have seen a marriage in maturity. In their more intimate sexual experience, in the greater security of the wife, in her playful freedom to initiate love, and finally in the fullness of their relationship the poet has sketched a revealing portrait of the model couple." (Glickman)

> iii. If we make the analogy to the relationship between Jesus and His people, then we can say that the words "**Make haste**" speak of her desire for His soon return. "I believe that our relationship to the Second Advent of Christ may be used as a thermometer with which to tell the degree of our spiritual heat. If we have strong desires, longing desires, burning desires, for the coming of the Lord, we may hope that

it is well with us; but if we have no such desires, I think, at best, we must be somewhat careless; perhaps, to take the worst view of our case, we are sadly declining in grace." (Spurgeon)

b. **And be like a gazelle or a young stag on the mountains of spices**: Previously the maiden thought of her beloved as *like a gazelle or a young stag upon the mountains of Bether*. Here the similar idea is connected with **mountains of spices**.

i. **Spices** speak of beauty, of fragrance, of value, of wealth, of sweetness; and these are **mountains of spices**! This was how great, how precious, how wonderful their relationship was to the maiden. No wonder she longed for his soon return.

ii. "The final invitation is to a continued celebration of the love and communion which the happy couple shares. The joys of physical union and mutual enjoyment are stamped with God's approval, for the Song of Songs is part of his holy Word." (Carr)

iii. "The figures of the deer and the mountains of spices symbolize for the last time the lover and his beloved. Restraints are gone. He is hers and she is his. They are free to pursue those delights of love that image a love to come for every believer." (Kinlaw)

Bibliography - Ecclesiastes & Song of Solomon

Carr, G. Lloyd *The Song of Solomon* (Leicester, England: Inter-Varsity Press, 1984)

Clarke, Adam *The Holy Bible, Containing the Old and New Testaments, with A Commentary and Critical Notes, Volume III – Job to Song of Solomon* (New York: Eaton and Mains, 1827?)

Deane, W.J. "Ecclesiastes," *The Pulpit Commentary, Volume 9 – Proverbs, Ecclesiastes, Song of Solomon* (McLean, Virginia: MacDonald Publishing, ?)

Eaton, Michael A. *Ecclesiastes* (Leicester, England: Inter-Varsity Press, 1983)

Estes, Daniel *Life and Love* (Schaumburg, Illinois: Regular Baptist Press, 1995)

Frankl, Viktor *Man's Search for Meaning* (New York: Simon and Schuster, 1959)

Glickman, S. Craig *A Song for Lovers* (Downer's Grove, Illinois: InterVarsity Press, 1980)

Kidner, Derek *A Time to Mourn, and a Time to Dance* (Downers Grove, Illinois: Inter-Varsity Press, 1976)

Kinlaw, Dennis F. "Song of Songs," *The Expositor's Bible Commentary, Volume 5* (Grand Rapids, Michigan: Zondervan, 1992)

Maclaren, Alexander *Expostions of Holy Scripture, Volume 3* (Grand Rapids, Michigan: Baker Book House, 1984)

Meyer, F.B. *Our Daily Homily* (Westwood, New Jersey: Revell, 1966)

Morgan, G. Campbell *Searchlights from the Word* (New York: Revell, 1926)

Morgan, G. Campbell *An Exposition of the Whole Bible* (Old Tappan, New Jersey: Revell, 1959)

Nee, Watchman *Song of Songs* (Fort Washington, Pennsylvania: Christian Literature Crusade, 1965)

Poole, Matthew *A Commentary on the Holy Bible, Volume 2* (London: The Banner of Truth Trust, 1968)

Spurgeon, Charles Haddon *The New Park Street Pulpit, Volumes 1-6* and *The Metropolitan Tabernacle Pulpit, Volumes 7-63* (Pasadena, Texas: Pilgrim Publications, 1990)

Taylor, J. Hudson *Union and Communion* (London: Morgan and Scott, ?)

Trapp, John *A Commentary on the Old and New Testaments, Volume 3 – Proverbs to Daniel* (Eureka, California: Tanski Publications, 1997)

Wright, Stafford J. "Ecclesiastes," *The Expositor's Bible Commentary, Volume 5* (Grand Rapids, Michigan: Zondervan, 1992)

As the years pass I love the work of studying, learning, and teaching the Bible more than ever. I'm so grateful that God is faithful to meet me in His Word.

Special thanks to Bob Romanelli who for the first time has helped me on a book with proofreading, suggestions, and editorial comments. Bob, I love you and the way you read these amazing books of Hebrew poetry!

Thanks to Brian Procedo for the cover design and all the graphics work.

Most especially, thanks to my wife Inga-Lill. She is my loved and valued partner in life and in service to God and His people.
David Guzik

David Guzik's Bible commentary is regularly used and trusted by many thousands who want to know the Bible better. Pastors, teachers, class leaders, and everyday Christians find his commentary helpful for their own understanding and explanation of the Bible. David and his wife Inga-Lill live in Santa Barbara, California.

You can email David at
david@enduringword.com

For more resources by David Guzik,
go to www.enduringword.com

www.ingramcontent.com/pod-product-compliance
Lightning Source LLC
LaVergne TN
LVHW011327080426
835513LV00006B/230